Neuro-Symbolic AI

Design transparent and trustworthy systems that understand the world as you do

Alexiei Dingli

David Farrugia

BIRMINGHAM—MUMBAI

Neuro-Symbolic AI

Associate Group Product Manager: Ali Abidi
Publishing Product Manager: Dinesh Chaudhary
Content Development Editor: Shreya Moharir
Technical Editor: Sweety Pagaria
Copy Editor: Safis Editing
Project Coordinator: Farheen Fathima
Proofreader: Safis Editing
Indexer: Hemangini Bari
Production Designer: Ponraj Dhandapani
Marketing Coordinators: Shifa Ansari and Vinishka Kalra

First published: May 2023

Production reference: 1190523

Published by Packt Publishing Ltd.
Livery Place
35 Livery Street
Birmingham
B3 2PB, UK.

ISBN 978-1-80461-762-5

www.packtpub.com

Dedicated with all my heart to my beloved family, my soulmate and wonderful wife Anna, and our precious children, Ben, Jake, and Faye. Your unconditional love, unwavering support, and endless encouragement have been the driving force behind my every achievement. To my parents, who instilled in me the values of hard work and perseverance, and to God, who has bestowed upon me the gift of knowledge and the opportunity to make a small but meaningful difference in the world. I am forever grateful and honored to dedicate this book to each and every one of you.

– Alexiei Dingli

To my family, who have always believed in me and pushed me throughout my journey. In particular, I want to dedicate this book to my sister, Tiziana, for her unwavering motivation, encouragement, and philosophical wisdom; and to my partner, Justine, for her countless sacrifices and constant support day in, day out. Thank you for always being there for me and inspiring me to be the best version of myself. This book is as much yours as it is mine.

– David Farrugia

Contributors

About the authors

Alexiei Dingli is a professor of AI at the University of Malta. As an AI expert with over two decades of experience, his research has helped numerous companies around the world successfully implement AI solutions. His work has been recognized globally, with international experts rating it as world-class. He is a recipient of multiple prestigious awards, including from the European Space Agency, the World Intellectual Property Organization, and the United Nations, to name a few. With a rich collection of peer-reviewed publications to his name, he is also an esteemed member of the Malta. AI task force, which was established by the Maltese government to propel Malta to the forefront of the global AI landscape.

David Farrugia is a seasoned data scientist and a PhD candidate in AI at the University of Malta. David Farrugia has worked in diverse industries, including gaming, manufacturing, customer relationship management, affiliate marketing, and anti-fraud. He has an interest in exploring the intersection of business and academic research. He also believes that the emerging field of neuro-symbolic AI has the potential to revolutionize the way we approach AI and solve some of the most complex problems in the world.

About the reviewers

Asim Munawar is a program director for neuro-symbolic AI at IBM Research, with a PhD in evolutionary algorithms from Hokkaido University. He has 15-plus years of experience with different AI technologies. He has led several research projects and customer engagements in various domains, including computer vision, robotics, acoustic analysis, and natural language processing. Asim is currently leading multiple projects to make large language models accessible to enterprise applications. He is interested in creating next-generation AI by combining symbolic knowledge and reasoning with data-driven learning methods. He holds 20-plus patents in the field of AI and has published more than 60 peer-reviewed articles.

Dr. André Meyer-Vitali is a computer scientist who got his PhD in software engineering, ubiquitous computing, and distributed AI from the University of Zürich. He has worked at the European Patent Office and on many applied research projects on ambient intelligence and multi-agent systems at Philips Research and **Netherlands Organization for Applied Scientific Research** (**TNO**) and contributed to AgentLink. Currently, he is a senior researcher at the **German Research Center for Artificial Intelligence** (**DFKI**), focusing on engineering and promoting Trusted AI, and is active in the AI networks TAILOR and CLAIRE. His research interests include software and knowledge engineering, design patterns, neuro-symbolic AI, causality, and **agent-based social simulation** (**ABSS**) with the aim of creating Trust by Design. André is also a passionate photographer.

Falk Pollok is a senior **software engineer** at IBM Research Europe and a senior **research software engineer** for the MIT-IBM Watson AI Lab, specializing in foundation models and multimodal question answering. Falk was a member of the MIT-Harvard-Stanford team on the **Defense Advanced Research Projects Agency's** (**DARPA**)'s **Machine Common Sense** project, contributed to IBM Watson Orchestrate, was the lead developer for IBM Sapphire and founded IBM's Engineering Excellence program. He holds a master's degree in **computer science** from RWTH Aachen, leadership certificates from Cornell, and IBM's highest developer profession rank. Moreover, he published eight papers in top conferences such as NeurIPS, AAAI, and Middleware, has two patents, was named a Face of IBM Research, and has received multiple awards, including IBM's **OTA** and InfoWorld's **Best of Open Source Software** (**BOSSIE**) award.

Table of Contents

5

Introducing Neuro-Symbolic AI – the Next Level of AI   83

6

A Marriage of Neurons and Symbols – Opportunities and Obstacles   99

7

Applications of Neuro-Symbolic AI   111

Preface

Neuro-symbolic **artificial intelligence** (**AI**) has become an increasingly critical area of study as it seeks to bridge the gap between human-like understanding and **machine learning** (**ML**) capabilities. Traditional AI has often struggled to grasp the nuances and complexities of human cognition, which is where neuro-symbolic AI comes into play. By combining the strengths of both neural networks and symbolic reasoning, this groundbreaking approach aims to design systems that understand the world as we do.

The main areas of focus in this book are as follows:

- The history and limitations of traditional AI
- The origins and evolution of symbolic AI and neural networks
- The principles and foundation of neuro-symbolic AI
- Practical applications and programming techniques for neuro-symbolic AI
- The need for explainable systems and the future of AI

In this book, we will take you on a journey through the evolution of AI. We will delve into the rise and fall of symbolic AI, followed by the neural networks revolution. Our exploration will then lead us to the exciting intersection of these two domains as we introduce neuro-symbolic AI as the next level of AI. Through the book, we aim to offer you a comprehensive understanding of the opportunities and challenges in the field of neuro-symbolic AI, as well as a practical guide to implementing some of these concepts in Python. We will also discuss the importance of explainable AI and the exciting future developments that await us. Rather than focusing solely on theoretical concepts, our book presents a balanced blend of theory, practical applications, and real-world examples. By using accessible language and detailed illustrations, we hope to make the topic engaging and approachable for both beginners and experienced AI enthusiasts alike.

Embark on this fascinating journey with us, and uncover the potential of neuro-symbolic AI to revolutionize the way we interact with intelligent systems. Let's explore how we can design systems that truly understand the world as we do and reshape the future of AI together.

Who this book is for

The book is aimed at data scientists, ML engineers, and AI enthusiasts who are looking to expand their knowledge of neuro-symbolic AI and stay up to date with the latest advancements in the field. The book covers all technicalities and provides introductory material for all aspects discussed in the book. However, a basic understanding of AI systems and programming is recommended, especially for the more technical chapters.

The key issues that this audience is facing include building powerful AI systems that are explainable, conscious of the domain, and can work without access to huge datasets. Therefore, the book will provide essential features, including a basic understanding of AI and a working knowledge of Python (and programming in general), to help address these challenges. By providing practical and hands-on examples, the book will also help you to overcome your fear of trying new AI experiments and apply the concepts learned in real-world applications.

What this book covers

Chapter 1, The Evolution and Pitfalls of AI, provides an introduction to the fundamentals of AI, its various types, uses, benefits, and limitations, as well as the mechanics of building AI systems.

Chapter 2, The Rise and Fall of Symbolic AI, discusses the concept of symbolic learning and its history, inner mechanics, and limitations.

Chapter 3, The Neural Networks Revolution, introduces neural networks, their types, potential use cases, and limitations.

Chapter 4, The Need for Explainable AI, highlights the motivation for **explainable AI (XAI)**, its importance, and the current state-of-the-art techniques.

Chapter 5, Introducing Neuro-Symbolic AI: The Next Level of AI, introduces the composite AI topic of neuro-symbolic AI, its mechanics, and its emergence as a way forward for AI development.

Chapter 6, A Marriage of Neurons and Symbols: Opportunities and Obstacles, explores the trade-offs between reasoning and learning and the benefits, challenges, and research gaps in neuro-symbolic computing.

Chapter 7, Applications of Neuro-Symbolic AI, showcases different neuro-symbolic AI applications based on different techniques, inspiring creativity in the adoption of this composite technology.

Chapter 8, Neuro-Symbolic Programming in Python, provides a basic programmatic outline to design and implement neuro-symbolic systems in Python.

Chapter 9, The Future of AI, discusses future developments of AI, the rise of **artificial general intelligence (AGI)**, and the ethical issues associated with the creation of singularity.

To get the most out of this book

The book covers all technicalities and provides material for all aspects discussed in the book. However, a basic understanding of AI systems and Python programming is recommended, especially for the more technical chapters. In some of the chapters, the book also assumes basic knowledge of first-order Boolean logic.

Software/hardware covered in the book	Operating system requirements
Python 3.7+	Windows, macOS, or Linux

If you are using the digital version of this book, we advise you to type the code yourself or access the code from the book's GitHub repository (a link is available in the next section). Doing so will help you avoid any potential errors related to the copying and pasting of code.

Download the example code files

You can download the example code files for this book from GitHub at `https://github.com/PacktPublishing/Neuro-Symbolic-AI`. If there's an update to the code, it will be updated in the GitHub repository.

We also have other code bundles from our rich catalog of books and videos available at `https://github.com/PacktPublishing/`. Check them out!

Download the color images

We also provide a PDF file that has color images of the screenshots and diagrams used in this book. You can download it here: `https://packt.link/94c17`.

Conventions used

There are a number of text conventions used throughout this book.

`Code in text`: Indicates code words in text, database table names, folder names, filenames, file extensions, pathnames, dummy URLs, user input, and Twitter handles. Here is an example: "Mount the downloaded `WebStorm-10*.dmg` disk image file as another disk in your system."

A block of code is set as follows:

```
html, body, #map {
  height: 100%;
  margin: 0;
  padding: 0
}
```

> **Tips or important notes**
> Appear like this.

Get in touch

Feedback from our readers is always welcome.

General feedback: If you have questions about any aspect of this book, email us at `customercare@packtpub.com` and mention the book title in the subject of your message.

Errata: Although we have taken every care to ensure the accuracy of our content, mistakes do happen. If you have found a mistake in this book, we would be grateful if you would report this to us. Please visit `www.packtpub.com/support/errata` and fill in the form.

Piracy: If you come across any illegal copies of our works in any form on the internet, we would be grateful if you would provide us with the location address or website name. Please contact us at `copyright@packt.com` with a link to the material.

If you are interested in becoming an author: If there is a topic that you have expertise in and you are interested in either writing or contributing to a book, please visit `authors.packtpub.com`.

Share Your Thoughts

Once you've read *Neuro-Symbolic AI*, we'd love to hear your thoughts! Scan the QR code below to go straight to the Amazon review page for this book and share your feedback.

`https://packt.link/r/1-804-61762-8`

Your review is important to us and the tech community and will help us make sure we're delivering excellent quality content.

Download a free PDF copy of this book

Thanks for purchasing this book!

Do you like to read on the go but are unable to carry your print books everywhere?

Is your eBook purchase not compatible with the device of your choice?

Don't worry, now with every Packt book you get a DRM-free PDF version of that book at no cost.

Read anywhere, any place, on any device. Search, copy, and paste code from your favorite technical books directly into your application.

The perks don't stop there, you can get exclusive access to discounts, newsletters, and great free content in your inbox daily

Follow these simple steps to get the benefits:

1. Scan the QR code or visit the link below

https://packt.link/free-ebook/9781804617625

2. Submit your proof of purchase
3. That's it! We'll send your free PDF and other benefits to your email directly

1

The Evolution and Pitfalls of AI

Artificial intelligence (**AI**) is considered by many as the new kid on the block, but in reality, it's more of an elderly person. Significantly, few people realize that the AI drive we're experiencing today started around the Second World War. Back then, people such as Vannevar Bush, John von Neumann, and Claude Shannon were very much toying with different ideas that eventually led to the creation of today's modern computers. However, it was Alan Turing, the famous British mathematician, who, after using a rudimentary computer during the war, started visualizing the potential of AI. After the Second World War, many other scientists came on board and eventually created the field of AI. The initial drive was toward using algorithms capable of manipulating symbols (such as alphanumeric characters) but eventually, these techniques hit a brick wall. In the past three decades, we have seen a steady shift toward a different kind of AI, called **statistical AI**. These algorithms are capable of achieving some incredible feats using large-scale statistical techniques. However, today, we are heading toward another crossroads. The limitations of these technologies are becoming visible. Even though a self-driving car can boast a driving experience of around 60 years of continuous driving, there have been cases where these cars were hacked by simply placing a small sticker on a traffic sign. These AI models do not understand how our world works and because of this, a simple hack can cause one of these cars to steer directly into a wall. Thus, we need better AI, one that is not only capable of maintaining the incredible performance achieved by **deep learning** (**DL**) models but is also able to understand our world and how it works.

This chapter aims to explore the evolution of AI so that you can appreciate its humble beginnings and the various achievements of the past decades. However, it is also important to understand that the path taken was not always a straight one and AI scientists had to face various obstacles along the way. By the end of the chapter, you will have a solid understanding of AI and the pitfalls it faced, and you will be able to have a better understanding of the AI ecosystem. In this chapter, we will cover the following main topics:

- The basic idea behind AI
- Subfields of AI
- The evolution of AI
- The pitfalls of AI

The basic idea behind AI

Even though many people do not realize it, they are at the mercy of AI. Today, we have doorbells, lighting, ovens, washing machines, air conditioners, cars, and all sorts of devices that we use on a daily basis having some AI integrated within them. The problem with AI is that these devices don't have a label on them that clearly shows whether an AI system is controlling them or not. Thus, my state-of-the-art appliance doesn't look much different from my old one, yet underneath the bonnet, they are worlds apart.

Most people's AI education has been heavily influenced by Hollywood movies or science fiction books. *A.I. Artificial Intelligence, I, Robot, Ex Machina, Blade Runner, The Matrix,* and *2001: A Space Odyssey,* to name a few, all contributed to building this general understanding of AI. Unfortunately, there seems to be a recurrent theme in all of them. First, AI is all about humanoid robots. Second, they must harm the human race in their quest for freedom. Unfortunately, both assumptions are rather far-fetched. Robotics is a subfield of AI, but a robot is essentially just a shell concealing the AI program, so much so that the bulk of AI research focuses on the software rather than the hardware. For the other part, at the moment, AI is not sentient. It cannot perceive or feel; it has no dreams or aspirations, and to be honest, AI researchers have no idea how to create an AI like that. So, unless we crack this problem and make a sentient machine, it is implausible that an AI would want to harm the human race in any way.

However, not everything is negative since books and movies allow different generations to dream and create their fantasy world about the future of technology. In 1962, the Jetsons animated sitcom launched, portraying a middle-class family of four who lived in Orbit City, a space town, in around 2062. Robotic maids roamed the town, undertaking errands for their masters, and people traveled using flying cars. While we're still not there, such shows conditioned people's expectations about the future.

In reality, there have been various advancements in the past years. While we don't have a robotic maid like in the Jetsons, we do have virtual assistants (such as Alexa, Siri, and Cortana) who can open the curtains for us in the morning, brew some excellent coffee, order food, switch on the TV set on our favorite Netflix show, and also instruct robotic vacuum cleaners to clean the house while we're sleeping. The point is that AI is designed to be ubiquitous. It is everywhere but non-invasive in such a way that the user doesn't realize that they're interacting with a computer. Unfortunately, this makes the understanding of AI somewhat complicated.

AI is a field of study that encompasses multiple disciplines (primarily, computer science) and aims to develop machines capable of intelligent behavior. The term *AI* is a combination of *artificial* and *intelligence. Artificial* refers to the fact that it is human-made and not naturally occurring, while *intelligence* is a complex concept that lacks a clear definition universally agreed upon. To get around this problem of definitions, Alan Turing, the grandfather of AI, came up with an ingenious idea to define intelligence via association. Humans are capable of labeling intelligent behavior. If we see an animal performing fun tricks that are normally attributed to a human, we say that the animal exhibited a level of intelligence. Machines are considered intelligent if they can do tasks that only intelligent entities or groups, such as humans or social creatures, can perform. AI is the field that focuses on creating machines that demonstrate intelligent behavior.

Since intelligent processes apply to all fields of study, AI can be considered a horizontal area that intersects with all the others. That is why its applications range from controlling a humble climate control system in a car to automating a nuclear power plant. Simple automation using if-then rules can be found on the lower end of the spectrum, while very complex algorithms based on how the human brain works are being developed for the most advanced functions. Today, AI has the ability to execute a wide range of tasks, improve various procedures, and forecast upcoming occurrences with a level of precision that is typically beyond human capabilities.

The use of AI can be highly beneficial for organizations, which is why many are now embracing this technology. With vast amounts of data at its disposal, an AI system can effectively examine it, uncover patterns, and instantly detect any problems. Furthermore, when it comes to monotonous or hazardous manual tasks, AI can automate them, thereby improving efficiency and safety. AI systems have various benefits over their human counterparts; they are precise in their work, don't get bored, they suffer no burnout, can foresee future trends, and are capable of handling much more data than a person can ever manage. That is why the World Economic Forum predicts that in a few years' time, automated systems will (for the first time in human history) surpass the number of humans working in industry.

Even though AI emerged out of computer science, there's a massive difference between the two. Creating intelligent software is not just about programming a computer to drive a car by obeying traffic rules. That is the easiest part. The biggest challenge is the learning aspect. We live in a world with imperfect information that is constantly evolving. Even though there are road guidelines, the width of the road might not be consistent. Road markings start fading with time. Even a perfect road is problematic if there's a sandstorm, heavy rain, fog, or even snow. An autonomous vehicle has to deal with these conditions and a million others, some of which we haven't even thought of! So, the only way to achieve that is by using learning algorithms that experience the real world and learn from it when they encounter different conditions. In fact, it is estimated that today's self-driving vehicles have a collective intelligence of more than 60 years of continuous driving, a feat rather impossible to achieve for any human being.

Although most people started to understand AI and its implications in the past decade, the underlying technology is not new and has been around for more than half a century. The term *artificial intelligence* was coined in 1956 during the Dartmouth Summer Research Project. Back then, a group of scientists led by Professor John McCarthy organized a two-month workshop aimed at brainstorming about intelligent applications of computers. They wanted to determine whether machines could learn like a young child, using trial and error or by developing some kind of formal reasoning. They wanted to find ways in which machines could "*use language, form abstractions and concepts, solve kinds of problems now reserved for humans, and improve themselves.*"

One of the things they realized during that workshop is that computers can actually achieve those tasks but it was not something that they could resolve in a few weeks. In fact, today, more than 60 years later, AI has become a massive field of study that branched into all the other academic disciplines. But it spent the major part of those years confined to university campuses and research labs around the world. It was only recently that it started seeping into the commercial world and influencing our daily lives. This occurred due to a number of factors:

- Given the proliferation of technology in all sorts and means, the amount of data created daily is unprecedented; so much so that 90% of the information found on the internet was generated in the past two years

- With the development of powerful processors, the invention of graphical processing units, and the rise of cloud technologies, computers can now process massive amounts of data in a very short time

- New algorithms were created that harness the power of novel architectures, thus allowing AI to achieve new heights

Notwithstanding this, we are still in the era of AI. By this, we are referring to that part of AI that is extremely good at dealing with a limited set of problems but fails miserably when given a simple problem that is slightly different. Just take the game of Go as an example. Go is a strategy board game invented in China around 2,500 years ago. The problem with Go is that it is so complex that the possible combinations in-game amount to around 2.082×10^{170}, which is more than all the atoms of the universe combined. Because of this complexity, computers weren't capable of winning against a human Go Grandmaster until 2015, when AlphaGo managed to reach the professional level without limitations. Ironically, even though AlphaGo was capable of this feat, if someone asks it for the current time in Beijing, it will get a little confused because it wasn't programmed for that function.

Note on AlphaGo

AlphaGo is a computer program developed by DeepMind Technologies, a subsidiary of Alphabet, designed to play the game of Go.

But these limitations are only temporary. Big corporations are already working on AI models capable of processing speech, images, and text simultaneously, such as the **data2vec** model recently released by Meta. This is all possible thanks to a subfield of AI normally referred to as **machine learning** (**ML**). It can be considered as the superstar of AI since it is practically used in all the other subfields. ML algorithms gather huge amounts of information, process it, and become smarter over time. Unlike humans, they do not suffer from memory loss, information overload, or other distractions. However, they're far from perfect since learning is a very difficult task, even for trivial tasks. Just consider the distinction between a cat and a dog. Humans are capable of learning the differences pretty quickly, accurately, and from a very young age. For a machine, it is much more difficult. We have to keep in mind that algorithms mainly consider physical appearance; they have no background knowledge and they don't even understand how the world works. So, just taking their appearance into account, we can say that dogs have floppy ears and cats have pointed ears, but this doesn't hold in all cases. Maybe we can consider the texture, the color, the patterns, the length of their tail, or several other features. But first of all, it's not a trivial task to program such a system because things get complicated rather quickly, and second, it will never be perfect. Thus, we need to find a way in which machines start learning from a handful of experiences – as any toddler does, after all. That is what ML systems do: they analyze hundreds of examples and train an algorithm. It is then tweaked over time and eventually, the algorithm becomes smarter. This is how we are achieving incredible results with self-driving cars, in pharmaceuticals when the COVID vaccine was created in record time, in Industry 4.0, and in thousands of other applications.

The way in which society is evolving is rather different than what was portrayed in Hollywood movies. AI will not be there to seek revenge on its human master but rather to help humans in their daily tasks. Because of this, our relationship with technology will change completely. Autonomous vehicles will not only operate a transport service but since people are not driving, they can use that time to have a meeting, take a nap, or even enjoy a television show. Eventually, AI will also affect some of the jobs we are used to today. In fact, the World Economic Forum estimates that around 85 million jobs will be displaced worldwide but AI will also create around 97 million new jobs. So, we must prepare ourselves for the world of tomorrow with up-skilling and re-skilling initiatives. While we cannot imagine the full ramifications of this technology, one thing that's for sure is that there will be a lot of disruption. But the most logical future is one where humans and AI work together to solve a problem and, ultimately, create a better world. AI will help us accomplish more tasks in a shorter amount of time, it will save us from having to do tedious repetitive tasks, and allow us to do what we do best: be human! Let's have a look now at how AI evolved, starting from humble beginnings up to becoming the most powerful technology ever invented by man.

The evolution of AI

In the previous section, we have seen that the term *AI* was coined back in 1956. But really and truly, as can be seen in *Figure 1.1*, AI is built on other areas whose development dates much earlier, almost to the dawn of mankind. We first meet records of automations in Homer's Iliad, where automatic door openings were described. In Ancient Egypt, statues of deities could move their heads to send signals to the people, while in Greek mythology, we find records of Hephaestus's automata, Talos the man of bronze, and the silver watchdogs of King Alkinous of the Phaiakians. Mankind has been dreaming of AI since the very beginning!

We have to keep in mind that AI is a multidisciplinary field of study made up of different bits and pieces brought forth from the intersection of different topics (see the following diagram):

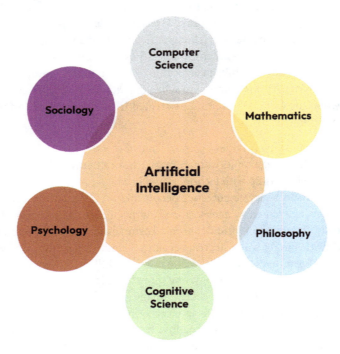

Figure 1.1 – Origins of AI

The following are the most important areas that contribute to AI:

- **Computer science** is the study of computers and computing systems. It essentially lays the foundation for AI.

- **Mathematics** is a science that deals with numbers and abstract concepts. Both CS and AI find their roots in mathematics. Whether we're talking about processing data, writing complex algorithms, or even displaying fancy virtual reality interfaces, everything is based on mathematics.

- **Philosophy** is the study of both fundamental and generic questions dealing with all sorts of topics including reasoning, organization of knowledge, mind models, and so on. As AI deals with a lot of conceptual problems in the quest of modeling our world, philosophy helps us to deal with and tackle these issues.

- **Psychology** is the study of the human mind and behavior. It's important to keep in mind that AI is an applied field and, in many circumstances, it has to deal with people. The most obvious example is the use of AI in social media, where the system has to identify the most interesting posts for the user.

- **Cognitive science** studies the thinking process of humans, which includes elements of learning, thought formulation, and information organization within the brain. AI scientists tend to borrow ideas from nature, so much so that the subfield referred to as **Artificial Neural Networks** is primarily devoted to simulating how the brain works.

- **Sociology** is a social science dealing with human behavior: patterns, relationships, interactions, and everyday life. With the rise of social networks, AI is extensively used to help people connect.

Of course, this was just a selection of the major topics and there are other disciplines that are important for AI. Finally, we should not forget that AI is really and truly a horizontal subject that can plug into almost all the other fields. Let's now have a look at the most important milestones in human history that contributed to the evolution of AI.

Philosophy

Let's start our journey from the very beginning, around 384 BC. We can imagine Socrates and Aristotle debating and coming up with the idea of formulating a precise set of laws. This is important for AI because, in our applications, we try to either recreate those laws (as in virtual worlds) or create agents that need to understand how the world works. However, this is not always possible because our world is based on fuzzy concepts that cannot be explicitly defined easily. Just to give you an example, imagine a chair; let's write a definition for the most basic form of a chair. Most probably, we would say it has four legs, a back to rest against, and a surface to sit on. Even though we know that not all chairs follow this definition, the majority of them probably do. However, a pertinent question arises: can we categorize a car as a chair? It has four legs (wheels), a back (windscreen), and a surface (bonnet). The obvious answer is that it isn't, even though it technically complies with our definition of a chair. The reason is not that it's not possible, because we all know that we can sit on top of a car but we don't usually do it. So, there are other unwritten rules that cannot be captured and that we learn through our interaction with society and the world. These rules are normally unknown to AI.

Moving on, around 1315, Ramon Lull came up with the idea of reasoning by mechanical artifacts. In those days, they even tried to create machines that were capable of reasoning. The idea was that if they were given a particular situation, they could reason upon the situation and come up with a plausible solution. This idea was also explored by Leonardo da Vinci when he designed the first mechanical calculator. By using such a device, one could perform simple calculations. Unfortunately, this device was ahead of its time and, in fact, was never created.

In 1588, Thomas Hobbes started toying with the idea of using mathematical thinking to model reasoning aspects. Another important person is without a doubt Blaise Pascal, a mathematician who created a calculator called the Pascaline. Around the same time, Gottfried Wilhelm Leibniz came up with something similar but it had a very subtle difference: rather than dealing with numbers, it dealt with concepts. This fact is important because we are moving up a level of abstraction. Those scientists were no longer dealing with numbers but with something tangible that we can visualize rather easily. Finally, we find Rene Descartes, who came up with the idea that the human mind is exempt from physical laws and pushed the idea of the soul. He used this to explain the element of free will. This was very important because we were now moving toward the idea of sentience. We started looking at machines that are independent of ourselves, machines that are capable of doing things beyond what the programmer actually instructs them to do, and that brings us to what AI is trying to pursue – the quest of creating autonomous machines capable of making their own decisions by going beyond their basic program.

Out of the various attempts at creating the first calculator, the most successful is probably by Charles Babbage, who came up with the idea of what he called the differential engine. Essentially, this was a machine capable of calculating some mathematics such as polynomial functions. Unfortunately, this engine wasn't really that successful and, in fact, some years later, he came up with an even bigger idea, which he called the analytical engine, which was capable of solving any mathematical function. An important aspect to note was that these were not simply calculators but they were also programmable machines. In fact, the person who used to program them was Lady Ada Lovelace, the daughter of the British poet Lord Byron, and Annabelle Milbank. She actually wrote programs for the differential engine and the analytical engine but unfortunately, since the engines never really worked, these programs couldn't be tried and tested. However, these machines laid the foundation for modern programming.

Logic

In logic, we try to develop precise statements about all things and their relationships. In fact, Aristotle uses the following example to illustrate this:

Logical Example:

Socrates is a man,

All men are mortal,

Therefore, Socrates is mortal.

In logic, given valid premises and sound logic, it will yield correct conclusions. However, the problem is that our world is not always so well defined. Just think about a very simple example: *What is the population of the United States?*

Possible answers include the following:

- 334,914,050 people
- Almost 350 million
- Less than India

Technically, they're all correct answers; however, they are not precise statements because it is very hard to come out with an exact number. But they are all still correct, so unfortunately, in our world, we have to accept a high level of uncertainty where the elements of truth are not always well defined. Logic is very important because machines can easily process it, so we have to find ways of translating our world into a format understood by these logical machines. In 1965, a program was created that could solve any solvable problem using logical notation within a well-defined world. This shows that even though our world has various constraints, if the rules of the world are well defined, we can actually use computers to solve the problems that exist. However, the biggest problem is always the initial one: how to define the world in such a way that it can be processed by machines. To try to overcome that issue, we tend to use informal logic to state the formal terms.

Mathematics

Mathematics can be described as the cornerstone on which AI is built. It started with the Persian mathematicians in 980 who created the first numerals and the first algebraic concepts. Closer to our time, we find George Boole who, in 1847, came up with the idea of Boolean logic. This logic is similar to what we've seen before but it is based upon a system having only two values, either true or false. This proved to be perfect for computers since they are composed of electrical switches that can only have two states, on or off. Eventually, Gottlob Frege generalized further on this concept and created first-order logic. The idea behind this is to move toward a higher level of abstraction that is much easier for humans to understand. With first-order logic, we are no longer bound to numbers but we can specify functions representing objects such as a car or fruit. This not only creates a link between numbers and the real world but also makes it incredibly easy for us to perform logical inferences on the constituents of our world.

At the time, the limits of mathematics were being explored, and Kurt Godel came up with the incompleteness theory. The theory states that in any language that is expressive enough to describe the properties of natural numbers, there are true statements that are undecidable.

In this completeness example, is the following sentence true or false?

This sentence is false.

If the sentence is true, then by using the same definition of the statement, it must be false. If the sentence is false, then by using the same definition of the statement, it must be true. Thus, we can never be certain about the validity of that statement, hence it is incomplete.

Alan Turing later also explored the undecidability problem: how can we know whether a program will finish or run forever? This is a huge problem. Let's imagine a software engineer is writing a program but they are unsure whether the algorithm will actually finish or whether it will keep on going forever without ever finding a solution. This can have great implications for the way we use computers. Because of that, it is important to prove whether our programs are undecidable or not.

Another important element is intractability. Sometimes, we have programs that have been running for a very long time and, of course, we need to know whether they will stop or not. With intractability, we can define problems that will take an incredible amount of time but we know that they are solvable. So, even if it takes hundreds of years, we know that, eventually, the program will stop.

Identifying whether an algorithm is undecidable or intractable is very important because it allows us to come up with solutions that will eventually finish or stop exploring others that have no solution. Remember that an intractable problem today (one that is very difficult to solve in reasonable time) may be solved in the future when we have more processing power. Chinese scientists have recently built a quantum computer [1] that could perform a computation within 3 minutes that would otherwise take around 10,000 years of processing power on our fastest super-computer. As you have just seen, the foundations of AI are based on mathematical concepts and that is why mathematics is extremely important.

Cognitive science

Cognitive science is another interdisciplinary science that draws from many fields, such as psychology, linguistics, and philosophy. It develops theories about human perception, thinking, and learning. It is used in AI because, with it, we can create cognitive models so we can try to understand how a person actually thinks, and using those models, we can come up with algorithms in order to mimic that thinking. It is also heavily used in the psychological part because we tend to deal with the interaction between machines and humans where psychological factors are extremely important. Furthermore, we try to create theories of the mind to understand how we learn about new concepts, what happens inside our brains, how we store those concepts, and how we reason upon them, especially when the concepts are very abstract and difficult to understand. By studying how our minds work, we can try to create algorithms that operate on similar principles.

A short history of AI

In the following sections, we'll have a look at the major milestones that defined modern AI to help us understand how this technological field developed in the past decades.

Second World War research

In 1942, Isaac Asimov, a science fiction writer, came up with the laws of robotics, which were published in the short story *Runaround*. There is the zero rule (which was introduced later) and the three main rules:

- A robot may not harm humanity or, by inaction, allow humanity to come to harm

- A robot may not injure a human being or, through inaction, allow a human being to come to harm

- A robot must obey any orders given to it by human beings, except where such orders would conflict with the first law

- A robot must protect its own existence as long as such protection does not conflict with the first and second laws

In 1943, Walter Pitts and Warren McCulloch came up with the idea of a neural network – a mathematical structure inspired by the inner workings of the brain made up of artificial neurons all connected together. They process the information and pass it to other neurons, thus instructing the different parts of the body to do a particular task.

In 1945, Vannevar Bush, head of the Scientific Research and Development office of the US during World War Two, came up with a description of the Memex. Essentially, it's a device in which individuals store all their books, records, and communications so that they may be consulted with exceeding speed and flexibility. Essentially, he foresaw the internet.

AI inception

In the 1940s, Alan Turing, the famous British mathematician, computer scientist, and father of AI, was posted at Bletchley Park during the Second World War. Together with other code breakers, he had to decode enemy messages. While there, he devised a number of techniques for speeding up the process of breaking the ciphers, and to help him, he created the Colossus, one of the first super-computers, which was instrumental to decode the German Enigma machine. It is estimated that, thanks to his work, the war in Europe was shortened by more than two years, thus saving the lives of more than 14 million people!

After the war, Turing kept on thinking about AI and devised the Turing Test – a test to see whether a computer can trick a person into believing that it is a person. He believed that if a human could not tell the difference between a computer and another human, then the computer can be considered intelligent on a par with a human.

In 1952, Arthur Samuel created the first ML program capable of playing checkers. The interesting part was that the program improved itself the more it played. Eventually, it also managed to challenge an amateur player.

In the summer of 1956, eminent computer scientists such as Marvin Minsky, Claude Shannon, John McCarthy, and others organized a summer workshop at Dartmouth where they coined the term *artificial intelligence*. The organizers of the workshop were optimistic that it would generate fresh perspectives and significant advancements in the field of AI. Their aim was to demonstrate that all facets of intelligence, including learning, can be precisely articulated such that machines can replicate them. The participants sought to explore ways of enabling machines to utilize language, develop abstractions and concepts, solve complex problems that were once the exclusive domain of humans, and enhance their own abilities. Of course, they didn't manage to solve all the challenges in two months, but it marked the birth of the AI field of study and its subfields.

Cold War developments

In 1962, the **Massachusetts Institute of Technology** (**MIT**) built a knowledge base chess-playing program called MacHack. It was good enough to take part in human tournaments and it managed to get ranked in class C.

1969 saw the development of a new algorithm called backpropagation, which is used to train neural networks. Even though it has some very obvious limitations, by the 1980s, this algorithm became quite standard in ML and is still in use today.

These were also the years of the Cold War between the US and Russia. The biggest threat in those years was a nuclear attack, so the US wanted to create a system capable of sending messages from one part of the country to the other, even if the connection was partially down (because of a nuclear bomb). Because of this, the foundations of the internet were laid down with the creation of the TCP/IP2 protocol, capable of sending messages across a vast dynamic network.

> **Note on TCP**
>
> **TCP** stands for **Transmission Control Protocol** and it deals with the transmission of data across the network. **IP** stands for **Internet Protocol**, which is essentially the indexing mechanism of how to reference a particular machine over the internet.

Another application that became necessary because of the Cold War was **machine translation (MT)**. It is the idea of getting a piece of text in one language and translating it into a different language. In those days, the Americans had a lot of Russian documents that they needed to translate quickly into English text. The algorithms of the time were very good at literally translating text, but we all know that literal translations are not always good. For example, if we take Mark 14:38 from the Bible (*the spirit is willing, but the flesh is weak*), the MT system returns *the vodka is good, but the meat is rotten*. Of course, that is not the intended meaning. But because of these failures, a lot of people lost interest in AI in general. This is also referred to as the first AI winter, a period of reduced funding and interest in AI research. There are several reasons why AI winters happen. One of the primary causes is unrealistic expectations, where AI is hyped up to be a magical solution to all problems, but when the technology does not live up to the hype, it leads to a decline in interest and funding. Another reason is a lack of breakthroughs or progress in the field, which can lead to a lack of interest and funding. Additionally, during times of economic uncertainty, companies and investors may cut back on funding for AI projects to focus on more pressing matters. Lack of available data, overregulation, and lack of public trust are other factors that can contribute to AI winters. Ultimately, AI winters occur due to a combination of technological, economic, and social factors.

Birth of the internet

The 70s also brought the birth of the internet. The network was originally financed by the **Defense Advanced Research Projects Agency (DARPA)** and called the **Advanced Research Projects Agency Network (ARPANET)**. Originally, there were only a few universities that were connected. In 1971, direct dialing was created and people could actually connect to the main server by simply dialing using a normal phone line. In 1972, the first public demonstration with 24 sites was launched. By 1973, there were connections with England and Norway, and the first satellite connection was established. A year later, the internet expanded to more than 62 computers online. Of course, today, around 22 billion computers are connected to the same global network. This development is critical for AI because the proliferation of connected devices and the growth of the World Wide Web has created a massive amount of data. ML algorithms rely on such data to train models and improve their performance, and the internet provides a way to access and process this data easily. Thus, it is considered as a critical infrastructure for the development and deployment of AI technologies.

Another important development around that period is SHRDLU, a computer program created by Terry Weingard (from MIT) that uses natural language understanding to control a simple 3D environment. The system is a simple simulation displaying a number of cuboids and other objects, such as pyramids. The user then gives natural language commands to move objects, name collections, or maybe query the state of the simplified block world. The incredible thing about SHRDLU is that it is a fully solvable system that can answer all the queries given. However, the limitation is that it is a closed-world environment so fairly limited. But this proves that if we can describe a world well enough, then we can easily create queries about anything within that world.

AI in commercial use

Around 1985, people started experimenting with computers that can actually talk. One of the first systems was called NetTalk, which was capable of learning like a child. It actually started babbling, and then slowly started forming various words. It was initially trained on around 10,000 words and improved gradually.

Unfortunately, this lack of progress led to the second AI winter. By now, AI had become a $3 billion industry; however, it started to collapse! The 80s was a very particular time for computing; companies started investing in large mainframe computers, and the personal computer craze just started. They were mass produced and their costs were extremely low. The 80s also saw the rise of expert systems, a massive database that collects information about specialized applications such as medical expert systems. These expert systems saved companies $2 million per year and they proved extremely useful; however, they served a very restricted domain. So, they couldn't be used for anything apart from the task they were built and designed for. Eventually, people started losing hope in AI again. This was a massive hit for the US and especially Japan, as they invested a lot of money in expert systems. Because of these failures, the funding for AI dried up once again.

The era of the World Wide Web

The early 90s saw the birth of the **World Wide Web** (**WWW**), the visual part of the internet. In 1991, Tim Berners Lee posted a note on an internet newsgroup defining two things: how a web server and a line browser operate. The line browser and the web server are two important components of the WWW. The line browser is the interface for people to actually access the internet (such as Safari, Chrome, Firefox, and others). The web server is the program that sends files to the browser. So, servers started appearing immediately after his post; the most popular at the time was Mosaic. In 1994, the World Wide Web Consortium was created whose task was to manage all the WWW protocols. A new language called the **HyperText Markup Language** (**HTML**) was created to define the layout and style of the content found on a web page.

In the late 90s, AI reached an important milestone. A powerful computer called Deep Blue (from IBM) played chess against the chess grandmaster, Garry Kasparov, and won. It was unheard of that a computer not only managed to win against a chess grandmaster but also became the top player in the world.

In 1998, Tim Berners Lee, together with some colleagues, came up with another idea that foresaw the next evolution of the web. At the time, it was referred to as the **Semantic Web**. The current WWW is aimed at human consumption so people can look at web pages, understand them, enjoy them, and have fun. However, those web pages are incredibly difficult for an AI to understand. So, the idea behind the Semantic Web was to infuse meaning inside the web. By doing so, AI systems can make use of the existing online content and build intelligent services on top of the current web.

Modern applications of AI

The new millennium also saw more ambitious applications of AI. The first humanoid robots made an appearance with Azimo, created by Honda. It was able to walk almost as fast as a human, do simple tasks such as deliver trays to customers in a restaurant setting, and do some simple cleaning.

2007 saw another important initiative that changed our world forever. DARPA launched the Grand Challenge for autonomous vehicles. It urged companies to create autonomous vehicles furnished with different sensors, capable of obeying traffic rules and operating in an urban environment. The sensors could detect cars that were approaching, people that were crossing the road, bicycles, traffic signs, and all the other elements found in our road network. In 2009, Google launched its first autonomous vehicle, and it started testing in the US. Today, self-driving cars can be found in different parts of the world, offering functions such as assisted drive, summoning, and autopilot.

In 2010, seven researchers at the University of Alberta managed to solve the game of checkers. The ultimate champion became an AI system capable of not only playing the game but also winning most of the time, eventually becoming the world champion.

In the last decade, there has been an accelerated adoption of AI in practically all imaginable fields. IBM's Watson not only managed to win Jeopardy, the famous TV game show, but is today used in large research projects ranging from weather forecasting to cancer research. Every one of us is today using some sort of AI, such as Google Home, Cortana, Alexa, or Siri. Essentially, we started the DL era and various organizations are now investing heavily in AI technologies.

The past decade also saw the evolution of DL technologies, with numerous breakthroughs propelling the field forward. The origins date back to the 80s when Yann LeCun pioneered the development of convolutional neural networks (CNNs) by creating a system capable of recognizing handwritten digits. The progress continued in 2012 when Geoff Hinton's team achieved state-of-the-art performance on the ImageNet dataset using CNNs trained on GPUs. A year later, in 2013, DeepMind made a leap by employing deep reinforcement learning to train an agent that could play Atari games. The introduction of the transformer architecture in 2016 revolutionized the field further, particularly in natural language processing. 2021 saw AlphaFold solving the protein folding problem, a longstanding challenge in molecular biology. Most recently, in 2022, ChatGPT, an advanced language model, was released to the public and quickly garnered over 10 million users within weeks, exemplifying the growing influence and impact of DL in various domains.

But there's a lot going on in this field and the following is a list of state-of-the-art technologies being developed at the moment by the major players:

Company	Technology	Description
DeepMind	Reinforcement learning	An ML method that learns like a child by rewarding desired behavior
OpenAI	Transformers	A neural network that learns context (through an attention mechanism) and tracks relationships among sequences of information
Facebook (now Meta)	Self-supervised learning	An ML process that uses a part of the input to train the model on itself
Google	AutoML	AutoML tries to democratize ML by using automation to apply it
Apple	Federated learning	An ML method that allows the algorithm to learn while preserving the privacy of the individual providing the data
Microsoft	Machine teaching	A process that adds context and business rules to AI training data to produce better results
Amazon	Transfer learning	Pre-training an ML model and using relevant parts of that model to solve similar problems
IBM	Quantum machine learning	A research area that explores the interaction of quantum computing and ML

Table 1.1 – State-of-the-art technologies developed by major players in the last decade

Notwithstanding these exciting developments, many researchers believe that DL technologies are reaching their limits. Because of this, there's a lot of research going on in order to find the next technology that will take us beyond the limitations of existing DL models.

Subfields of AI

Now that we've explored the origins of AI and understood how it evolved over the years, let's look at the different subfields that constitute this vast field of study. At this stage, it's important to note that there isn't a single subdivision acceptable to everyone. There might be other ways of dividing these areas, and some might also overlap. However, this is an attempt at logically organizing the subfields of AI.

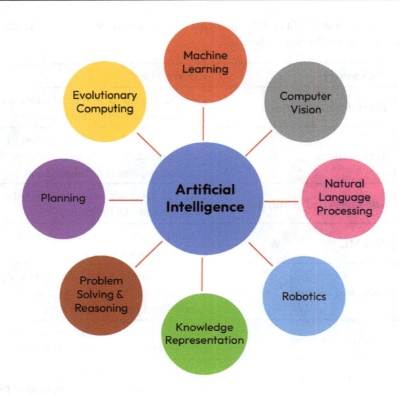

Figure 1.2 – Subfields of AI

ML

ML tries to create algorithms capable of learning. It typically starts by using data found in a training set and then generates predictions out of that data. DL is one of the various subfields of ML, which tries to create learning algorithms while gaining inspiration from the brain's inner workings. Today, this subfield is considered the superstar of AI, and in fact, it is used in almost all the other subfields. ML has various applications such as email filtering, pharmaceuticals, security, and so on.

Computer vision

Computer vision (CV) deals with extracting information from images or videos. Essentially, it tries to mimic the human visual system using a computer. The process involves gathering images, processing them, analyzing the various aspects, understanding their content, and transforming them into descriptions that make sense. CV has multiple applications, such as understanding the inputs in a self-driving car, the visual inspection of microscopic components in an electronics manufacturing plant, or the processing of gigabytes of images obtained from the James Webb Space Telescope.

Natural language processing

Natural language processing (**NLP**) is a subfield of AI and linguistics concerned with understanding natural languages such as English, Italian, and Mandarin. It deals with the whole process starting with converting speech to text, analyzing the text, understanding it, generating new text, and converting it back to speech. Many users are familiar with this technology since they interact with chatbots or personal assistants (such as Siri) and use translation algorithms regularly. However, in the near future, there will be a proliferation of NLP since it provides a natural interface for humans, one which they learned when they were still young.

Robotics

Robotics is maybe the most known subfield of AI. It has been portrayed in various Hollywood movies, thus fueling popular imagination. The subfield deals with the design, construction, and operation of computers capable of interacting with our physical 3D world. Although robots are not widespread yet, there are many successful examples that have penetrated our homes, such as vacuum cleaner robots, curtain openers, and delivery bots. On the higher end, we can find autonomous vehicles and a suite of advanced robots by Boston Dynamics, including Atlas (a humanoid as agile as a person), Spot (a quadruped robot similar to a dog), and Handle (a wheeled robot with an arm).

Knowledge representation

Knowledge representation is a more theoretical subfield of AI with various implications for all the other subfields. Essentially, it deals with the problem of representing our world inside a computer. As we've seen in different sections, this is not a trivial task but an essential one. If we cannot represent all the objects in our world with their relationships, we cannot create robots or self-driving cars that understand what's around them and how to deal with it.

Problem-solving and reasoning

Problem-solving and reasoning involve the ability to generate a hypothesis, identify the intermediary steps, and reach a sensible solution. It is typically divided into two: the ability to define a problem and effectively find a quick solution to that problem. Such a subfield affects most of the other applications in one way or another since problem-solving is an integral part of interacting with our world.

Planning

Planning seeks to explore ways of using autonomous techniques to tackle planning problems. By doing so, it tries to optimize the overall performance of the system. It is also more abstract than problem-solving and reasoning because usually, a plan might involve different steps over time and be based upon other triggering conditions. A typical example might be an AI system that performs vacation route planning. It not only needs to create a plan that covers different locations across different times (in a reasonable way) but it also needs to adjust the plan according to dynamic events (such as weather conditions, accidents, or diversions).

Evolutionary computing

Evolutionary computing is a subfield of AI used to solve complex optimization problems. As its name suggests, these algorithms are inspired by biological evolution and, in fact, they use genetic operators (such as parental selection, crossover, mutation, and fitness). There are various applications for these algorithms, such as machine scheduling, allocation of constrained resources, and generating strategies in a multi-agent environment.

The pitfalls of AI

Sometimes, it is easy to get caught up in the AI hype, and we can get the impression that AI can solve all the problems of the world. It is essential to analyze AI pitfalls because they can help us understand what's real and what's not, and what works and what doesn't.

Is AI limitless?

When we look at different AI applications, many are simply amazing: self-driving cars, pizza delivery drones, machine-brain interfacing, and so many others. But have we ever stopped and asked ourselves whether they are ready for use or whether they're just a concept? Because unfortunately, many of these amazing applications are created in a lab but they're not commercialized, yet people make a lot of hype about them. So, there's a thin line between what is production-ready and what isn't. When looking at different applications, you have to do some due diligence, speak with experts, and try to understand the current state of the art with regard to AI. It is imperative to keep in mind that AI has its limitations and we have to understand and work around those limitations. Having said that, in most cases, AI manages to find partial solutions for a lot of problems. But still, we have to keep in mind those limitations because they might affect our solutions.

How important is the data?

If you were to have a look at the new algorithms that have been developed in the past two decades, you would realize that they consume a lot of data. While older algorithms did not use so much data, their performance in comparison to the new ones was very limited, and this is why they were not as successful as the new breed of DL algorithms. Because of that, if we want to increase the performance of our applications, we have to provide large amounts of appropriate data. So before embarking on a project, AI scientists have to think about the data and check whether they have enough and whether it is the correct type of data. So, we have to be extremely careful about the data issue and analyze the data before we even start considering AI projects.

Can we get training data?

We should not worry if we do not have adequate data, as there are different ways in which we can try to obtain various sorts of data. Imagine we have the task of trying to identify and recognize house numbers. Of course, there are different variations, including different numbers, colors, sizes, and shapes, and some are written as words while others are written as numerals. So, the basic idea here is to try to recognize these numbers. To train an AI algorithm, we need a good training set; to create it, we need to collect these numbers. There are various approaches we can use, but the following are a few examples:

- Go around (in a car or by walking) and take pictures of different house numbers. This is what Google did when they needed to collate all the Street View images from around the world. They bought cars, placed a camera on top of them, and the cars went around most roads to take pictures and videos of different streets worldwide. This is how the Google Street View project came about.

- If that approach is not possible (maybe due to budget restrictions), scientists can use synthetic data created in a lab. For example, in a case study, we need to recognize different numbers, so a program that uses different fonts, sizes, colors, and so on generates an extensive sample data collection. Using synthetic data, we can quickly boost our training set, which helps us train the AI.

- Another approach we can take is to use the little data we might have and create new instances out of that data. A simple way to do so is by rotating the images. We can also skew them, flip them, or even change their color. By doing so, we will generate new data points, which will help the algorithm learn and understand different numbers.

- The last approach makes use of transfer learning, which is a technique that uses data from different domains and applies it to the current application, thus avoiding the cold-start problem. An example would be an AI system trained to translate between two popular natural languages (such as English to Spanish) and then used to teach a model for a low-resource language (such as English to Maltese). So, by using transfer learning, researchers can quickly inflate a training set and pump it up to get better results.

However, it's important to remember that these approaches do not necessarily work in all situations. However, in most cases, we can manage to find a solution to our problem using similar techniques. Since the provision of data is a big problem for AI, there's a lot of research to try to solve this issue with as little data as possible.

Have we got good data?

While many companies using computerized systems probably have access to large quantities of data, it's essential to remember that not all data is good. So, we have to be sure that the information is satisfactory. If humans look at pictures of cats and dogs, it is straightforward to distinguish which is which, but if the data is not labeled, then it is tough to train an AI algorithm on that data. Having large quantities of data without the required meta information is rather useless.

But even if we have this information, not all pictures are the same. Just look at *Figure 1.3*, showing photos of chihuahua dogs and muffins. It is challenging for a machine to distinguish between the two. So, the quality of the data is paramount.

Figure 1.3 – DL approach for a very similar object recognition application on chihuahuas and muffins
(source: Enkhtogtokh Togootogtokh, Amarzaya Amartuvshin (CC BY 4.0))

But even if we have good data, we must ensure that the data is balanced and has a good representation of the different classes we want to identify. Let's consider the cats and dogs example mentioned earlier. We cannot have a dataset of images representing 10% dogs and 90% cats because it will be challenging for an algorithm to learn the differences between them. While this is a toy example to illustrate the problem, there can be much more severe consequences.

In 2015, Amazon created a hiring tool that uses AI, and when they tested it out, it immediately started discriminating against women. After examining the issue, they found out that their system was biased because they trained their AI algorithms to look for potential candidates who had a similar resume to those that already worked at the company. When teaching their system, they did not realize that since tech companies have a 75% male-dominated workforce, they inadvertently introduced the bias. So, Amazon's AI system taught itself that male candidates were preferred; it penalized resumes with certain words with female connotations and preferred candidates who littered the resume with masculine-associated verbs. The dangers of having a biased dataset are real and can lead to discrimination. We have to be very careful what we feed to AI algorithms because, otherwise, if the data is wrong, then the prediction of the AI algorithm will also be wrong.

Can a high-performance AI still fail?

The simple answer is *Yes*. Even though precision and accuracy indicate that the AI is working, they don't necessarily validate that the AI is working well. A recent study conducted at the University of Washington developed a classifier that could differentiate between images of wolves and huskies. The model was trained on various concepts and tested on a new dataset. It was surprising that despite the similarities between huskies and wolves, the system achieved nearly 90% accuracy. The researchers were pleased with the results until they used an explainer function to understand why the algorithm performed so well. They discovered that the model relied heavily on the background, rather than the foreground, to distinguish between the two animals. The photos of wolves were typically captured in the wild with a snowy background, while husky images had less snow in the background. Consequently, the researchers realized that they had created a reliable snow detector instead of a wolf versus husky classifier. The issue is not apparent when evaluating performance measures such as accuracy or precision. In conclusion, while AI has undoubtedly brought about significant advancements in various industries, it also poses several pitfalls that must be addressed. It is crucial for developers, policymakers, and society as a whole to work collaboratively to ensure that AI is developed and implemented responsibly to avoid potential negative consequences.

Summary

In this chapter, we looked at AI and how it evolved from humble beginnings until today, taking the world by storm. Through the different stages, we saw how AI slowly started seeping into various applications and leaving its mark, even where people traditionally reigned supreme. The chapter also introduced us to the different subfields of AI and briefly explained their contribution to the bigger picture.

Finally, we skimmed through various AI pitfalls, thus helping us realize that even though AI is a very powerful technology, it also has several limitations. This is why we need to seek new, more powerful alternatives, and this new hope seems to rely on a combination of statistical and symbolic AI.

But before delving further into it, in our next chapter, we will look at the rise and fall of symbolic AI so that we can understand what it is, before exploring the new field of neuro-symbolic AI.

2

The Rise and Fall of Symbolic AI

The Second World War saw massive scientific contributions and technological advancements. Innovations such as radar technology, the mass production of penicillin, and the jet engine were all a by-product of the war. More importantly, the first electronic computer (Colossus) was also developed to decipher encrypted Nazi communications during the war. After the war, the desire to achieve machine intelligence continued to grow.

As humans, we wanted to enable computers with human-like abilities. The primary motivation behind **Artificial Intelligence** (**AI**) systems has always been to allow computers to mimic our behavior, to enable machines to think like us and act like us, to be like us. Over the years, this motivation has remained virtually unchanged. However, the methodology and the mindset of how we approach AI has gone through several phases throughout the years.

While today, we rely on deep **Neural Networks** (**NNs**) (also known as Connectionism AI) to allow a machine to automatically teach itself how to solve a particular task, early AI systems were heavily ruled, and logic-based methods were used to teach computers human behavior. These systems are referred to as Symbolic AI. **Symbolic AI** is one of the earliest forms of AI. In his 1985 book *Artificial Intelligence: The Very Idea*, John Haugeland coined **Good Old-Fashioned AI** (**GOFAI**) as a reference to Symbolic AI. It dominated the computer science and AI fields from the 1950s all the way through to the 1970s. One of the first successful implementations of Symbolic AI dates to 1951, when Christopher Strachey, a British computer scientist, wrote over 2,000 instructions to teach a computer how to play the game of checkers (draughts). Today, Symbolic AI has been leveraged to solve many problems, including **Natural Language Processing** (**NLP**) applications and **Expert System** (**ES**) implementations.

This chapter aims to understand the underlying mechanics of Symbolic AI, its key features, and its relevance to the next generation of AI systems.

The first objective of this chapter is to discuss the concept of Symbolic AI and provide a brief overview of its features. Symbolic AI is heavily influenced by human interaction and knowledge representation. We will discuss how this shaped Symbolic AI. We will then examine the key features of Symbolic AI, which allowed it to dominate the field during its time. After that, we will cover various paradigms of Symbolic AI and discuss some real-life use cases based on Symbolic AI. We will finally discuss the main challenges when developing Symbolic AI systems and understand their significant pitfalls.

This chapter will go through the following topics:

- Defining Symbolic AI

- Knowledge representation through symbols and signs

- Critical features of Symbolic AI

- The different paradigms and applications of Symbolic AI

- Limitations and pitfalls of Symbolic AI

Let us get started with defining what we mean by Symbolic AI.

Defining Symbolic AI

Symbolic AI, GOFAI, or **Rule-Based AI** (**RBAI**), is a sub-field of AI concerned with learning the internal symbolic representations of the world around it. The main objective of Symbolic AI is the explicit embedding of human knowledge, behavior, and "thinking rules" into a computer or machine. Through Symbolic AI, we can translate some form of implicit human knowledge into a more formalized and declarative form based on rules and logic.

> **Understanding explicit and implicit knowledge**
>
> Explicit knowledge is any clear, well-defined, and easy-to-understand information. Explicit knowledge is based on facts, rules, and logic. An excellent example of explicit knowledge is a dictionary. In a dictionary, words and their respective definitions are written down (explicitly) and can be easily identified and reproduced.
>
> Implicit knowledge refers to information gained unintentionally and usually without being aware. Therefore, implicit knowledge tends to be more ambiguous to explain or formalize. Examples of implicit human knowledge include learning to ride a bike or to swim. Note that implicit knowledge can eventually be formalized and structured to become explicit knowledge. For example, if learning to ride a bike is implicit knowledge, writing a step-by-step guide on how to ride a bike becomes explicit knowledge.

In the Symbolic AI paradigm, we manually feed knowledge represented as symbols for the machine to learn. Symbolic AI assumes that the key to making machines intelligent is providing them with the rules and logic that make up our knowledge of the world.

Humans, symbols, and signs

Symbolic AI is heavily inspired by human behavior. Humans interact with each other and the world through symbols and signs. The human mind subconsciously creates symbolic and subsymbolic representations of our environment. It's how we think and learn. Our world is full of fuzzy implicit knowledge. Objects in the physical world are abstract and often have varying degrees of truth based on perception and interpretation. Yet somehow, we can still knowingly navigate our way through life. We can share information and teach each other new skills. We can do this because our minds take real-world objects and abstract concepts and decompose them into several rules and logic. These rules encapsulate knowledge of the target object, which we inherently learn.

This approach has been our way of life since the beginning of time. Thomas Hobbes, a British philosopher, famously said that thinking is nothing more than symbol manipulation, and our ability to reason is essentially our mind computing that symbol manipulation. René Descartes also compared our thought process to symbolic representations. Our thinking process essentially becomes a mathematical algebraic manipulation of symbols. Think about it for a second. What happens when we think? We start to formulate ideas. Ideas are based on symbols that represent some other object. For example, the term *Symbolic AI* uses a symbolic representation of a particular concept, allowing us to intuitively understand and communicate about it through the use of this symbol. Then, we combine, compare, and weigh different symbols together or against each other. That is, we carry out an algebraic process of symbols – using semantics for reasoning about individual symbols and symbolic relationships. Semantics allow us to define how the different symbols relate to each other. They also enable us to interpret symbolic representations.

To properly understand this concept, we must first define what we mean by a **symbol**. The Oxford Dictionary defines a symbol as a *"Letter or sign which is used to represent something else, which could be an operation or relation, a function, a number or a quantity."* The keywords here *represent something else*. Symbols are merely explicit references to implicit concepts. We use symbols to standardize or, better yet, formalize an abstract form. This process is also commonly referred to as **conceptualization**. At face value, symbolic representations provide no value, especially to a computer system. However, we understand these symbols and hold this information in our minds. In our minds, we possess the necessary knowledge to understand the syntactic structure of the individual symbols and their semantics (i.e., how the different symbols combine and interact with each other). It is through this conceptualization that we can interpret symbolic representations.

Let's consider a newborn child, for example. At birth, the newborn possesses limited innate knowledge about our world. A newborn does not know what a car is, what a tree is, or what happens if you freeze water. The newborn does not understand the meaning of the colors in a traffic light system or that a red heart is the symbol of love. A newborn starts only with sensory abilities, the ability to see, smell, taste, touch, and hear. These sensory abilities are instrumental to the development of the child and brain function. They provide the child with the first source of independent explicit knowledge – the first set of structural rules.

With time and sensory experiences, these structural rules become innate to the human mind, promoting further psychological development. The child begins to understand and learn rules – such as if you freeze water, it will eventually become ice. Here, ice is purely a label representing frozen water. Fire is hot, and if you touch *hot*, it will hurt. The child will begin to understand the physical and psychological world one rule at a time, continuously building the *world's symbolic representation* by learning newer and perhaps more complex syntactic and semantic logical rules. Eventually, the child will be able to communicate these symbolic representations with other humans and vice versa. As humans, we widely encourage the formalization of knowledge. Therefore, we are entirely dependent on symbolic knowledge. Some symbolic examples include the following:

- **Phonograms**: Any symbol (typically a letter or character) used to represent vocal sounds or linguistics (or both). Phonograms are used to describe the pronunciation of a particular word. For example, the term *dog* has the phonogram *d/o/g (3)*, while the word *strawberry* has the phonogram *s/t/r/aw/b/err/y (7)*.

- **Logograms**: Any linguistic symbol (a letter or sign) that is used to represent any complete word or phrase. Logograms do not consider the phonetics of the said word or phrase. The *$* (dollar) and *&* (ampersand) signs are good examples of logograms.

- **Pictograms**: Any schematic graphical (pictorial) symbol representing an entire word, phrase, or concept. Gender symbols and graphical charts are two examples of pictograms.

- **Typograms**: Any symbol, typically linguistic, that represents the definition or implication of a particular word through manipulating its letters. A typogram essentially becomes a symbol that encapsulates another symbol. For example, a typogram of the word *missing* might be *m-ss-n-g*. This is because the *"i"'s* are *missing* from the word.

- **Iconograms**: Any graphical symbol that is used to represent an entire word, phrase, or concept. Iconograms differ from pictograms because they tend to be more graphically and artistically detailed. A drawing of a flower or a view of a map are examples of iconograms.

- **Ideograms**: Any symbol that represents a word or concept. Ideograms are often in geometric shapes, which differ from other graphical symbols. As the name suggests, while they can define words, they are typically used to represent ideas. Examples of ideograms include a traffic stop sign or a no smoking sign.

Irrespective of our demographic and sociographic differences, we can immediately recognize Apple's famous bitten apple logo or Ferrari's prancing black horse. Even our communication is heavily based on symbols.

Figure 2.1 depicts the Sumerian language, which is recognized as being the first human language, dating back to circa 3100 BC (source: `https://www.history.com/topics/ancient-middle-east/sumer#:~:text=The%20Sumerian%20language%20is%20the,for%20the%20next%20thousand%20years.`). Its alphabet comprised graphical symbols representing various nouns, objects, and actions of the time. This is perhaps the best representation of the "thinking in symbols" concept.

Figure 2.1: The Sumerian language. Image by Mariusz Matuszewski on Pixabay

Humans thrive on interaction, and formalizing and declaring representations of implicit concepts and abstract objects is crucial to universal communicative abilities. The ability to create symbolic representations of the world around us might be a differentiating trait of intelligence. Recently, scientists have also found that other animals, including primates, dolphins, and horses, could understand and utilize human symbols to interact and communicate with humans. In one of their experiments, a group of horses was shown three symbols representing "no change," "add a blanket," and "remove a blanket." The horses could choose what they wanted based on the weather conditions by pointing toward the respective symbol. This feat is truly remarkable and drives the point home of the power behind symbols!

Now that we've discussed the vital role that symbols and signs play in everyday life, how does all this tie together with Symbolic AI?

Enabling machine intelligence through symbols

This symbolic philosophy was highly influential in the field of AI. The first examples of AI programs, such as the Logic Theorist (an AI program written in 1956 by Allen Newell, Herbert A. Simon, and Cliff Shaw that was able to prove theorems on the same level as a human mathematician) and the General Problem Solver (an AI programmed in 1957 by Herbert A. Simon, J. C. Shaw, and Allen Newell that used symbolic rule representations of problem knowledge as input to solve general tasks), involved symbolical processing in conquering the quest of achieving machine intelligence.

The concept of intelligence

Before we proceed any further, we must first answer one crucial question – what is intelligence? At face value, this question might seem relatively simple to answer. However, the term **intelligence** is complex to define. Intelligence tends to become a subjective concept that is quite open to interpretation.

Consider a popular TV talk show. In one of its popular segments, the host introduces two prodigy children: A and B. Child A can solve every mathematical problem in the world in record time. Child B can understand and speak every language like it's their native tongue. The host starts by introducing the audience to child A and, for the sake of entertainment, asks the child to solve a couple of math problems, each increasing in difficulty. The child answers correctly every time, and the audience is stunned and speechless. Everyone is in awe of this child's intelligence. Then, child B is also brought out by the host. The host asks child B to solve the same math problems as child A. Child B is not able to solve them correctly. The audience is not impressed. Is child B intelligent? To the audience, probably not. But to anyone who has witnessed the skills of child B, then probably the answer would be a strong and resounding yes.

> *"Everybody is a genius, but if you judge a fish by its ability to climb a tree, it will live its whole life believing it's stupid."*
>
> *– Unknown author (commonly misattributed to Albert Einstein)*

What is the takeaway here?

The definitions of intelligence, while being super subjective, essentially become a direct association and measure of the following:

- The problem we are trying to solve
- The context and environment of that problem

Although it is complex to define, humans subconsciously understand that intelligence is directly measured by how well you can do the task you are interested in. Intelligence is associated with reducing the significance and effect of our target problem. So, if we want a machine to be intelligent, it must solve a specific problem or task. But how can we teach the machine to solve a task? As we previously mentioned, early forms of AI were all about enabling computers to mimic human behavior. In short, it would allow machines to think.

Humans think in symbols. Computers operate using symbols. Therefore, computers can be thought to think.

Our journey through symbolic awareness ultimately significantly influenced how we design, program, and interact with AI technologies.

Towards Symbolic AI

Symbolic AI allows a machine to manipulate symbols about our world. The premise behind Symbolic AI is using symbols to solve a specific task. In Symbolic AI, we formalize everything we know about our problem as symbolic rules and feed it to the AI. Note that the more complex the domain, the larger and more complex the knowledge base becomes.

Symbolic AI leverages factual logic computation and comparison. Symbolic AI is more concerned with representing the problem in symbols and logical rules (our knowledge base) and then searching for potential solutions using logic. In Symbolic AI, we can think of **logic** as our **problem-solving technique** and **symbols and rules** as the means to **represent our problem**, the input to our problem-solving method. The natural question that arises now would be how one can get to logical computation from symbolism. We do this by defining symbol relations.

Understanding symbolic relations

Relations allow us to formalize how the different symbols in our knowledge base interact and connect. For example, let us consider a hamburger. The basic hamburger is a patty in between a bun. In this case, our symbols representing the object are BUN and PATTY. The relation would then be BETWEEN. We can define this symbolic relation as BETWEEN(PATTY, BUN).

We typically use predicate logic to define these symbols and relations formally – more on this in the *A quick tangent on Boolean logic* section later in this chapter.

Let us pick the task of determining whether an object is an orange or not as an analogy. When we see an orange or any other entity, we immediately dissect it and split it into its more minor constituents – its respective symbols. We use all our senses to build the knowledge base of the orange. For example, some properties of the profile that we consider might include the following:

- Shape
- Size
- Texture
- Color
- Body
- Origin

Figure 2.2 illustrates how one might represent an orange symbolically.

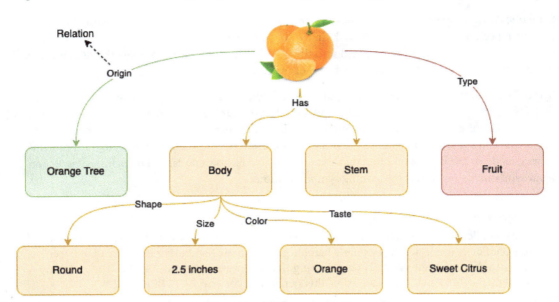

Figure 2.2: A symbolic representation of an orange

We observe its shape and size, its color, how it smells, and potentially its taste. We feel its texture and investigate its structure. In short, we extract the different symbols and declare their relationships. With our knowledge base ready, determining whether the object is an orange becomes as simple as comparing it with our existing knowledge of an orange. For example, we know that an orange should be orange in color. An orange should have a diameter of around 2.5 inches and fit into the palm of our hands. An orange resembles a round object with a stem emerging from its top. We learn these rules and symbolic representations through our sensory capabilities and use them to understand and formalize the world around us.

From symbols and relations to logic rules

So far, we have discussed what we understand by symbols and how we can describe their interactions using relations. The final puzzle is to develop a way to feed this information to a machine to reason and perform logical computation. We previously discussed how computer systems essentially operate using symbols. More specifically, computer processing is done through Boolean logic.

A quick tangent on Boolean logic

Any variable that can be either TRUE (1) or FALSE (0) is said to be a Boolean variable. A computer system comprises multiple digital circuits, with components with an input voltage that is either ON (i.e., state 1) or OFF (i.e., state 0).

In Boolean logic, we evaluate and compute a set of logical propositions (also called expressions) whose final output can be TRUE or FALSE. Logical propositions use *three* leading **logical operators** (logic gates) – AND, OR, and NOT:

- AND: All propositions must be TRUE for the entire proposition to be TRUE. We multiply the values of the propositions.

- OR: At least one of the propositions must be TRUE for the entire proposition to be TRUE. Then, we add the values of the propositions.

- NOT: Reverses the state of the logical proposition. If it is FALSE, it will become TRUE.

For a logical expression to be TRUE, its resultant value must be greater than or equal to 1. If the result is 0, then the expression is said to be FALSE.

There are some other logical operators based on the leading operators, but these are beyond the scope of this chapter.

Predicate logic 101

Predicate (first-order) is a formal system heavily used in multiple domains, including computing, discrete mathematics, and philosophy. We use predicate logic to define and represent expressions and statements in a standardized way. We use the symbol : = to denote a definition. On the left-hand side of the symbol is what we are trying to define, and on its right is the definition. We use the symbol ∧ to represent the AND operator, ∨ to denote the OR operator, and to replace the NOT operator. Given these three core operators, we can construct other operators due to functional completeness. For example, the NAND operator combines the AND and NOT operators. There are other symbols, such as the implication symbol (⇒). The AND, OR, and NOT operators are enough for this chapter. If the concept of predicate logic is new to you, we recommend you read more about this system.

Consequently, for a computer system to understand and process our symbolic relations, we must transform them into logical propositions. We can do this by adding logical operators to our symbolic relations. We typically refer to the logical operators as logical connectives since they connect all our symbols and their respective relations. For the sake of simplicity, let us pick a dummy example to understand this better. Consider the following statement:

```
People watch interesting and engaging movies
```

Given a specific movie, we aim to build a symbolic program to determine whether people will watch it. At its core, the symbolic program must define what makes a movie watchable. Then, we must express this knowledge as logical propositions to build our knowledge base. Following this, we can create the logical propositions for the individual movies and use our knowledge base to evaluate the said logical propositions as either TRUE or FALSE.

Step 1 – defining our knowledge base

The first step is to understand the problem we are trying to solve. Then, our problem becomes the world that we need to model. Finally, we can define our world by its domain, composed of the individual symbols and relations we want to model.

If we recall the original statement, we know that for people to watch a specific movie, the movie must be both interesting AND engaging. Therefore, let us tabulate and categorize the different components of the statement:

Symbols	Relations	Logical Connectives
PEOPLE MOVIES	WATCH INTERESTING ENGAGING	AND

Table 2.1: Statement dissected into its respective symbols, relations, and logical connectives

This step is vital for us to understand the different components of our world correctly. Our target for this process is to define a set of predicates that we can evaluate to be either TRUE or FALSE. This target requires that we also define the syntax and semantics of our domain through predicate logic.

Our symbols here are People and movies. They are our statement's primary subjects and the components we must model our logic around. Following this, we must define their binary relations.

- People watch movies
- A movie can be interesting
- A movie can be engaging

It is also an excellent idea to represent our symbols and relationships using predicates. In short, a predicate is a symbol that denotes the individual components within our knowledge base. For example, we can use the symbol M to represent a movie and P to describe people. We can also represent relations using predicates. A predicate relationship can have one or more arguments. Let us formally define the preceding relations.

Our first relation is that people watch movies. We can denote people watching movies using the WATCH predicate symbol. In this case, WATCH accepts two arguments: people and movies. Therefore, we can write this down as WATCH(P, M). Next, we have two other relations that accept only a single argument. These two relations define a property that a movie can possess. We can write them as IS_INTERESTING(M) and IS_ENGAGING(M).

Furthermore, the final representation that we must define is our target objective. Let us represent IS_INTERESTING(M) with I and IS_ENGAGING(M) with E.

Using first-order logic, we can define our target T as $T = I \land E$:

```
T is TRUE if both I and E are also TRUE
```

Let us also denote two movies – X and Y:

- Movie X is not interesting but engaging (therefore, $X = I \land E$)

- Movie Y is interesting and engaging (therefore, $Y = I \land E$)

Recall our target objective – i.e., to determine whether a person will watch the movie. We can formally write this inference rule as an implication as follows:

```
Person(P) AND Movie(M) AND IS_INTERESTING(M) AND IS_ENGAGING(M) =>
WATCH(P, M)
```

If we have a person, P, and a movie, M, where the movie is both interesting and engaging, then that implies the person will watch the movie.

Step 2 – evaluating our logical relations

So far, we have defined our domain regarding symbols and relations. The next step is to build our truth table to evaluate the validity of our expressions:

	I	E	T
Movie X	FALSE	TRUE	FALSE
Movie Y	TRUE	TRUE	TRUE

Table 2.2: Logical relation evaluation using a truth table

Based on our knowledge base, we can see that movie X will probably not be watched, while movie Y will be watched. Of course, this is a trivial example to get the message across.

Defining the knowledge base requires skills in the real world, and the result is often a complex and deeply nested set of logical expressions connected via several logical connectives. Compare the orange example (as depicted in *Figure 2.2*) with the movie use case; we can already start to appreciate the level of detail required to be captured by our logical statements. We must provide logical propositions to the machine that fully represent the problem we are trying to solve. As previously discussed, the machine does not necessarily understand the different symbols and relations. It is only we humans who can interpret them through conceptualized knowledge. Therefore, a well-defined and robust knowledge base (correctly structuring the syntax and semantic rules of the respective domain) is vital in allowing the machine to generate logical conclusions that we can interpret and understand.

Nonetheless, a Symbolic AI program still works purely as described in our little example – and it is precisely why Symbolic AI dominated and revolutionized the computer science field during its time. Symbolic AI systems can execute human-defined logic at an extremely fast pace. For example, a computer system with an average 1 GHz CPU can process around 200 million logical operations per second (assuming a CPU with a RISC-V instruction set). This processing power enabled Symbolic AI systems to take over manually exhaustive and mundane tasks quickly.

So far, we have defined what we mean by Symbolic AI and discussed the underlying fundamentals to understand how Symbolic AI works under the hood. In the next section of this chapter, we will discuss the major pitfalls and challenges of Symbolic AI that ultimately led to its downfall.

The fall of Symbolic AI

In the early 1980s, most AI developers moved away from Symbolic AI. Symbolic AI spectacularly crashed into an AI winter since it lacked common sense. Researchers began investigating newer algorithms and frameworks to achieve machine intelligence. As a result, Symbolic AI lost its allure quite rapidly. Furthermore, the limitations of Symbolic AI were becoming significant enough not to let it reach higher levels of machine intelligence and autonomy. In the following subsections, we will delve deeper into the substantial limitations and pitfalls of Symbolic AI.

Common sense is not so common

In a nutshell, Symbolic AI has been highly performant in situations where the problem is already known and clearly defined (i.e., explicit knowledge). Symbolic AI heavily relies on explicit symbolic representations. However, the world around us is filled with implicit knowledge. Our universe is a rather abstract concept. Translating our world knowledge into logical rules can quickly become a complex task. While in Symbolic AI, we tend to rely heavily on Boolean logic computation, the world around us is far from Boolean. Most physical symbols and relations are fuzzy. They are not static but rather based on a degree of truthiness. For example, a digital screen's brightness is not just on or off, but it can also be any other value between 0% and 100% brightness. A person can be a little hungry as opposed to completely starving. The concept of fuzziness adds a lot of extra complexities to designing Symbolic AI systems. Due to fuzziness, multiple concepts become deeply abstracted and complex for Boolean evaluation.

Additionally, it introduces a severe bias due to human interpretability. Let's pick a simple analogy – the color cyan. For some, it is cyan; for others, it might be aqua, turquoise, or light blue. As such, initial input symbolic representations lie entirely in the developer's mind, making the developer crucial. Recall the example we mentioned in *Chapter 1* regarding the population of the United States. It can be answered in various ways, for instance, less than the population of India or more than 1. Both answers are valid, but both statements answer the question indirectly by providing different and varying levels of information; a computer system cannot make sense of them. This issue requires the system designer to devise creative ways to adequately offer this knowledge to the machine.

Inevitably, this issue results in another critical limitation of Symbolic AI – common-sense knowledge. The human mind can generate automatic logical relations tied to the different symbolic representations that we have already learned. Humans learn logical rules through experience or intuition that become obvious or innate to us. They tend to come to us naturally, without us overthinking them. For example, a child must always be younger than their parents. We close our eyes when we want to sleep. We do not eat food that smells like it has gone bad. These are all examples of everyday logical rules that we humans just follow – as such, modeling our world symbolically requires extra effort to define common-sense knowledge comprehensively. Consequently, when creating Symbolic AI, several common-sense rules were being taken for granted and, as a result, excluded from the knowledge base. As one might also expect, common sense differs from person to person, making the process more tedious.

In the real world, there are so many different levels of abstraction, hierarchies, and underlying relationships. It's impossible to capture all these rules entirely. To start, even humans do not know all the universe's secrets. Let us recall the orange example from *Figure 2.2*. Assume we pass two fruits to the Symbolic AI program: an orange and a tangerine. With the symbolic structure and relations we had previously defined, it would be rather difficult to differentiate between them. Even a human might find this task difficult, let alone a machine that feeds knowledge through logical rules devised by a human.

Although Symbolic AI paradigms can learn new logical rules independently, providing an input knowledge base that comprehensively represents the problem is essential and challenging. The symbolic representations required for reasoning must be predefined and manually fed to the system. With such levels of abstraction in our physical world, some knowledge is bound to be left out of the knowledge base.

The test of time

Another concept we regularly neglect is time as a dimension of the universe. As we all know, time changes a lot of things. Some examples are our daily caloric requirements as we grow older, the number of stairs we can climb before we start gasping for air, and the leaves on trees and their colors during different seasons. These are examples of how the universe has many ways to remind us that it is far from constant.

A Symbolic AI system is said to be monotonic – once a piece of logic or rule is fed to the AI, it cannot be *unlearned*. Newly introduced rules are added to the existing knowledge, making Symbolic AI significantly lack adaptability and scalability. One power that the human mind has mastered over the years is adaptability. Humans can transfer knowledge from one domain to another, adjust our skills and methods with the times, and reason about and infer innovations. For Symbolic AI to remain relevant, it requires continuous interventions where the developers teach it new rules, resulting in a considerably manual-intensive process. Surprisingly, however, researchers found that its performance degraded with more rules fed to the machine.

We might teach the program rules that might eventually become irrelevant or even invalid, especially in highly volatile applications such as human behavior, where past behavior is not necessarily guaranteed. This phenomenon is referred to as concept drift or data morphism. In short, the underlying relationships of the data shift or change. Even if the AI can learn these new logical rules, the new rules would sit on top of the older (potentially invalid) rules due to their monotonic nature. As a result, most Symbolic AI paradigms would require completely remodeling their knowledge base to eliminate outdated knowledge. This remodeling process often becomes highly convoluted and tedious. For this reason, Symbolic AI systems are limited in updating their knowledge and have trouble making sense of unstructured data.

Symbolic AI today

Being the first major revolution in AI, Symbolic AI has been applied to many applications – some with more success than others. Despite the proven limitations we discussed, Symbolic AI systems have laid the groundwork for current AI technologies. This is not to say that Symbolic AI is wholly forgotten or no longer used. On the contrary, there are still prominent applications that rely on Symbolic AI to this day and age. We will highlight some main categories and applications where Symbolic AI remains highly relevant.

Expert systems

Symbolic AI has been predominantly used to design and develop ESs. IBM's **Representation, Ontology, Structure, Star** (**ROSS**) is a great example. You can refer to `https://arxiv.org/pdf/1411.4192.pdf` for further reading. ROSS is an expert system platform for legal research, much like an AI lawyer. Given a natural language prompt, ROSS can sift through the law, complete court cases, and other documents, and return relevant structured data and evidence based on the query. Symbolic AI is the core method behind several other expert systems, with additional examples being decision-making systems, process monitoring, and logistics.

Natural language processing

Symbolic AI was also seriously successful in the field of NLP systems. We can leverage Symbolic AI programs to encapsulate the semantics of a particular language through logical rules, thus helping with language comprehension. This property makes Symbolic AI an exciting contender for chatbot applications. Symbolical linguistic representation is also the secret behind some intelligent voice assistants. These smart assistants leverage Symbolic AI to structure sentences by placing nouns, verbs, and other linguistic properties in their correct place to ensure proper grammatical syntax and semantic execution.

Moreover, Symbolic AI allows the intelligent assistant to make decisions regarding the speech duration and other features, such as intonation when reading the feedback to the user. Modern dialog systems (such as ChatGPT) rely on end-to-end deep learning frameworks and do not depend much on Symbolic AI. Similar logical processing is also utilized in search engines to structure the user's prompt and the semantic web domain.

Constraint satisfaction

Naturally, Symbolic AI is also still rather useful for constraint satisfaction and logical inferencing applications. The area of constraint satisfaction is mainly interested in developing programs that must satisfy certain conditions (or, as the name implies, constraints). Through logical rules, Symbolic AI systems can efficiently find solutions that meet all the required constraints. Symbolic AI is widely adopted throughout the banking and insurance industries to automate processes such as contract reading. Another recent example of logical inferencing is a system based on the physical activity guidelines provided by the **World Health Organization** (**WHO**). The knowledge base of this AI is the guidelines themselves. Since the procedures are explicit representations (already written down and formalized), Symbolic AI is the best tool for the job. The researchers were able to provide the guidelines as logical rules. When given a user profile, the AI can evaluate whether the user adheres to these guidelines.

Explainable AI

Symbolic AI is also highly interpretable. Since the program has logical rules, we can easily trace the conclusion to the root node, precisely understanding the AI's path. For this reason, Symbolic AI has also been explored multiple times in the exciting field of **Explainable Artificial Intelligence** (**XAI**). A paradigm of Symbolic AI, **Inductive Logic Programming** (**ILP**), is commonly used to build and generate declarative explanations of a model. This process is also widely used to discover and eliminate physical bias in a machine learning model. For example, ILP was previously used to aid in an automated recruitment task by evaluating candidates' **Curriculum Vitae** (**CV**). Due to its expressive nature, Symbolic AI allowed the developers to trace back the result to ensure that the inferencing model was not influenced by sex, race, or other discriminatory properties.

These limitations of Symbolic AI led to research focused on implementing sub-symbolic models.

The sub-symbolic paradigm

Contrasting to Symbolic AI, sub-symbolic systems do not require rules or symbolic representations as inputs. Instead, sub-symbolic programs can learn implicit data representations on their own. Machine learning and deep learning techniques are all examples of sub-symbolic AI models.

Sub-symbolic models can predict some target objectives after extracting patterns from their input. Their training process is more significant than that of the manual symbolic process. With specific techniques, such as NNs, the developer does not even have to process the input data!

Sub-symbolic AI models can be scaled to more significant tasks and datasets effortlessly. Furthermore, sub-symbolic systems learn polytonic relationships, allowing for retraining and updating their previous knowledge. As such, sub-symbolic systems work well with non-stationary datasets. We tabulate the main differences between symbolic and sub-symbolic models as follows:

	Symbolic	Sub-Symbolic
Knowledge base	Manually defined symbolic rules and relations.	Automatic extraction using mathematical models.
Knowledge updates	It depends on the model complexity but is typically manually exhaustive.	Re-training of the model. Typically, an easy process but depending on use cases might be resource exhaustive.
Model development	A manually exhaustive process that tends to be rather complex to capture and define all symbolic rules.	Building the model and training is straightforward.
Missing data	Directly affects the performance of the model.	Can generally deal with missing or incomplete datasets.
Model upkeeping	A challenging and manual process.	Easy.
Model processing efficiency	Sequential evaluation of symbolic rules (slow).	Can be parallelized and scaled up (fast).
Result interpretability	Full traceability.	Ambiguous and complex to interpret.

Table 2.3: A comparison between the symbolic and sub-symbolic paradigms

Comparing both paradigms head to head, one can appreciate sub-symbolic systems' power and flexibility. Inevitably, the birth of sub-symbolic systems was the primary motivation behind the dethroning of Symbolic AI. Symbolic AI quickly faded away from the spotlight. Funnily enough, its limitations resulted in its inevitable death but are also primarily responsible for its resurrection.

As we got deeper into researching and innovating the sub-symbolic computing area, we were simultaneously digging another hole for ourselves. Yes, sub-symbolic systems gave us ultra-powerful models that dominated and revolutionized every discipline. But as our models continued to grow in complexity, their transparency continued to diminish severely. Today, we are at a point where humans cannot understand the predictions and rationale behind AI. Take self-driving cars, for example. Do we even know what's going on in the background? Do we understand the decisions behind the countless AI systems throughout the vehicle? Like self-driving cars, many other use cases exist where humans blindly trust the results of some AI algorithm, even though it's a black box.

Symbolic AI provides numerous benefits, including a highly transparent, traceable, and interpretable reasoning process. So, maybe we are not in a position yet to completely disregard Symbolic AI. Maybe Symbolic AI still has something to offer us. Throughout the rest of this book, we will explore how we can leverage symbolic and sub-symbolic techniques in a hybrid approach to build a robust yet explainable model.

Summary

Symbolic AI is one of the earliest forms based on modeling the world around us through explicit symbolic representations. This chapter discussed how and why humans brought about the innovation behind Symbolic AI. The primary motivating principle behind Symbolic AI is enabling machine intelligence. Properly formalizing the concept of intelligence is critical since it sets the tone for what one can and should expect from a machine. As such, this chapter also examined the idea of intelligence and how one might represent knowledge through explicit symbols to enable intelligent systems.

Knowledge representation and formalization are firmly based on the categorization of various types of symbols. Using a simple statement as an example, we discussed the fundamental steps required to develop a symbolic program. An essential step in designing Symbolic AI systems is to capture and translate world knowledge into symbols. We discussed the process and intuition behind formalizing these symbols into logical propositions by declaring relations and logical connectives.

Finally, this chapter also covered how one might exploit a set of defined logical propositions to evaluate other expressions and generate conclusions. This chapter also briefly introduced the topic of Boolean logic and how it relates to Symbolic AI.

We also looked back at the other successes of Symbolic AI, its critical applications, and its prominent use cases. However, Symbolic AI has several limitations, leading to its inevitable pitfall. These limitations and their contributions to the downfall of Symbolic AI were documented and discussed in this chapter. Following that, we briefly introduced the sub-symbolic paradigm and drew some comparisons between the two paradigms. These comparisons serve as a foundation for the rest of the book.

The following chapters will focus on and discuss the sub-symbolic paradigm in greater detail. In the next chapter, we will start by shedding some light on the NN revolution and examine the current situation regarding AI technologies.

Further reading

You can browse the following material for further reading to complement this chapter:

- Vellino, Andre. (1986). *Artificial intelligence: The very idea*: J. Haugeland (MIT Press, Cambridge, MA, 1985); 287 Artificial Intelligence. 29. 349–353.

- Cassirer, E. (1953). *The philosophy of symbolic forms*. New Haven: Yale University Press.

- For further information on Boolean logic and predicate logic, you can use these links:

  - `https://computer.howstuffworks.com/boolean.htm`

  - `https://www.tutorialspoint.com/discrete_mathematics/discrete_mathematics_predicate_logic.htm`

3

The Neural Networks Revolution

People have been fascinated with the inner workings of the brain for thousands of years. The first records can be traced back to a 1700 BC Egyptian papyrus, which reports the medical information of a person with a severe head injury. In Ancient Greece, Alcmaeon concluded that the brain is the organ that rules the body rather than the heart (as people thought back then) and that it also serves as the store for memories and thoughts. Furthermore, he also linked the eyes to vision processing inside the brain. Herophilus and Erasistratus of Alexandria even went a step further by distinguishing between the different components of the brain. During the Roman Empire, the Greek philosopher Galen started associating functions with the different brain parts and theorized about the function of the spinal cord. Around 1000 AD, Al-Zahrwai, the father of modern surgery, delved deeper into the inner workings of the brain. He evaluated neurological patients and treated head injuries. In Persia, Avicenna, the father of modern medicine, wrote a medical encyclopedia that, for the first time, associated mental health issues with the inner workings of the brain. During the Renaissance, Andreas Vesalius noticed the different specializations of the brain associated with different nerve cells. In the mid-18th century, Luigi Galvani observed the role of electricity in the brain to control nerves. And with the invention of the microscope, the study of the brain took a whole new dimension.

As we can see, the path was rather long and winding, spanning thousands of years. This led us to the creation of the first artificial neuron. In 1943, Warren McCulloch, a neurophysiologist, and Walter Pitts, a mathematician, wrote a paper describing how a neuron might work. And to prove their line of thinking, they recreated a single neuron using an electrical circuit. In the book *The Organization of Behavior*, Donald Hebb came up with the idea that neural pathways get strengthened when they are used, thus reinforcing the most preferred paths. Following this, IBM researchers started devising ways of simulating a neural network in their research lab. But the real boost came after the Dartmouth workshop in 1956, which pushed this field of study to new heights.

By 1958, the neurobiologist Frank Rosenblatt started modeling a physical perceptron. It was used to classify a stream of inputs into two distinct classes by computing the weighted sum of the inputs, removing a threshold, and passing one of the values as a result. A year later, Stanford researchers created MADALINE, the first neural network used to solve a real-world problem, and it was so successful that it's still being used today.

However, not everything was positive. In the book *Perceptrons* by Marvin Minsky and Seymour Papert, they proved that the perceptron is somewhat limited since it cannot mimic complex functions properly. This brought a slowdown in the development of neural network research since researchers were fearful that they might have hit a brick wall. Such a sentiment persisted till the early 80s.

In 1985, there was a new revival for **artificial neural networks (ANNs)**. Funding started flowing, annual meetings were organized, and in 1987, the **Institute of Electrical and Electronics Engineers' (IEEE)** first International Conference on Neural Networks attracted almost 2,000 attendees. Since then, ANNs have grown in strength and become incredibly intricate, spanning several layers, each with thousands of neurons. These complex networks can achieve incredible feats, from labeling images to controlling self-driving cars, or even translating text – in some cases, as well as if not better than humans.

In this chapter, we will cover the following topics:

- The basic idea behind artificial neural networks
- Different types of neural networks
- The complexities and limitations of neural networks

Artificial neural networks modeling the human brain

As we've just seen, large interconnected neural networks help us process information and model the world around us. In simple terms, as can be seen in *Figure 3.1*, a neuron gathers information from others using the dendrites, sums up all the inputs, and if the resultant value is beyond a certain threshold, it fires. This signal is then sent to connecting neurons through the axon. So, the dendrites are our input, the nucleus inside the neuron is where the processing happens, and the axon is our output.

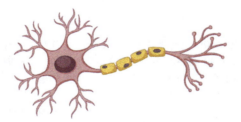

Figure 3.1: The neuron (Designed by brgfx/Freepik)

If we were to translate the concepts behind the neuron as illustrated in *Figure 3.1* to a computer, we would have a structure similar to the diagram in *Figure 3.2*. Essentially the dendrites are represented by the input nodes and there can be various inputs (X_1, X_2, X_3, …, and X_n). Since each physical dendrite might have different strength, this is represented in the ANN as a weight (W_1, W_2, W_3, …, and W_n) associated with each of the inputs. The operations inside the nucleus are represented by the summation and activation function, while the axon is the output link.

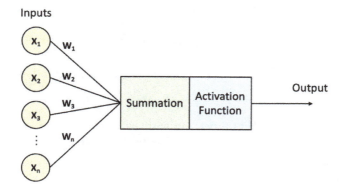

Figure 3.2: Model of a perceptron

In synthesis, a perceptron comprises weights, summation, and an activation function. When it receives an input, each one is individually weighted and combined using the summation process. The activation function then decides whether the signal should be sent to the output or not. Such perceptrons are also called **feed forward** (**FF**) because they receive inputs on the left and forward the values to the right. A very simple one is a step function that outputs 1 or 0, depending on whether a particular threshold is reached. However, this is only an example, and there exist several other functions, such as the sigmoid, Tanh, and **Rectified Linear Unit** (**ReLU**).

A simple artificial neural network

Let's have a look at a simple example. Imagine we need to create a neural network that detects whether a leaf is healthy or sick. The general rule is that brown spots next to the stem indicate some sort of illness. Take a look at the following diagram:

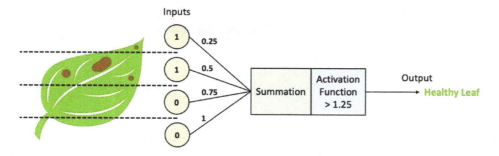

Figure 3.3: Example ANN for a healthy leaf

As per *Figure 3.3*, first, we divide the leaf into four sections, and if we notice a brown patch in that section, we set the corresponding input to 1; otherwise, we leave it as 0. The weights have been set up beforehand based on the function we're trying to model, so weights closer to the stem have a value of 1, and the furthest away have a value of 0.25. To calculate the input and weights, it's simply a matter of multiplying them together and sending them to the summation function to add them up:

```
( 0 x 1 ) + ( 0 x .75) + ( 1 x 0.5 ) + ( 1 x 0.25) = 0.75
```

The activation function decides whether the perceptron should fire or not. In this case, the rule is that if the value of the summation is greater than 1.25, then the leaf is sick.

> **Calculation tip**
> 1.25 is half of all the values possible. Imagine all the inputs were 1 (presence of brown spots), when we multiply them with the weights, we get (1 x 1) + (1 x .75) + (1 x 0.5) + (1 x 0.25) = 2.5, and half of 2.5 is 1.25.

But our summation gave us a value of 0.75, which is less than the threshold, therefore the perceptron will not fire, meaning that the leaf is healthy. If we repeat the same process but this time with a different leaf, as per *Figure 3.4*, we can see that the input varies since the brown patches are located closer to the stem. By calculating the input and weights and sending them to the summation function, we get the following:

```
(1 x 1) + (0 x 0.75) + (0 x 0.25) = 1.75
```

Since the result is greater than 1.25, the perceptron will fire, indicating that the leaf is sick.

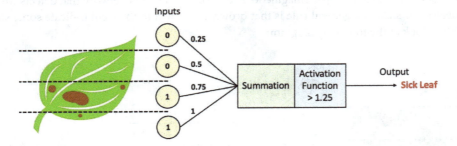

Figure 3.4: Example ANN for a sick leaf

The input part is relatively easy to understand. The complex part is the perceptron, regarding the selection of the weights, the aggregation, and the activation function. The way to do this is via learning. If we train a child to recognize a sick leaf, we will show them different examples and teach them the features used to identify its health. Following that, the child is then shown a new unseen leaf, and we can check whether the child learned the underlying concept or not. To train a perceptron, the same idea is used.

The problem with such an approach is that the perceptron is somewhat limiting. Keep in mind that the activation function acts like a dividing line. Anything below the threshold is rejected, and the rest is accepted. These are known as **linearly separable functions**. But most problems cannot be solved using such a simple mode.

Figure 3.5 shows a neural network that decides whether it should give a child sweets or ice cream. However, what happens if we add a simple rule that says that a child can choose either/or, but cannot select both? So, in one sitting, the child can either have sweets or ice cream, but not both. At this stage, the perceptron breaks because such a rule cannot be represented.

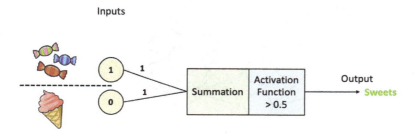

Figure 3.5: Example ANN to decide whether to give either sweets or ice cream, but not both

If we look at *Figure 3.6*, which shows all the available options, we find that it is impossible to draw a straight line from one end to the other, which allows us to specify that all options on one side of that line are valid while the others are not. This is because a linearly separable function cannot represent such a process on its own.

Figure 3.6: The four options (nothing, sweets only, ice cream only, and no sweets or ice cream) of the sweets and ice cream function

To go around this limitation, we can simply add various perceptrons together into a multilayered neural network, as per *Figure 3.7*. The main difference is that the previous model made up of inputs, perceptron, and outputs is changed, whereby instead of one perceptron, we can have several. These are generally referred to as the *hidden layers of an ANN*.

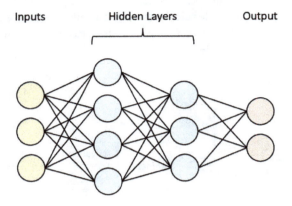

Figure 3.7: A multilayer perceptron

In a typical ANN, one would find several hidden layers, and each layer can have any number of nodes. However, such a setup increases the complexity of the ANN, and because of this, determining the correct weights (especially in the hidden layers) becomes extremely difficult. Luckily for us, in the 1970s, an algorithm called **backpropagation** was created to do just that!

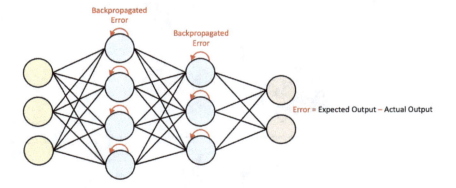

Figure 3.8: The backpropagation process

The concept behind backpropagation is relatively simple, as can be seen in *Figure 3.8*. When we start training the ANN, the weights are set randomly. When we give it an input, this will inevitably give us wrong results (due to the incorrect weights). We then compare the wrong result obtained in the output layer with the expected output and, from the difference, calculate the errors. Then, we simply take the errors and propagate them back to the hidden layers while adjusting the weights slightly throughout the process. By doing so, the error gradually decreases. The process is then repeated several times until we reach a state in which the error is so tiny that it is negligible, thus indicating that the ANN is correctly representing the function being modeled. Thus the network is unable to improve any further.

In this section, we have seen the most basic ANN architectures; the single-layer perceptron (*Figure 3.2*) and the multilayer perceptron (*Figure 3.7*). However, many others are much more complex than what we've seen so far. In the next section, we will explore a few of the most popular ANN architectures.

Introducing popular neural network architectures

In this chapter, we explore some of the most popular ANN architectures beyond the basic single-layer and multilayer perceptrons. The **recurrent neural network** (**RNN**) is a feed-forward network that incorporates temporal relationships and is widely used in applications ranging from sentence autocompletion to stock market predictions. However, RNNs suffer from the vanishing gradient problem, which hinders their learning ability. Competitive networks, such as Kohonen networks and self-organizing maps, classify inputs without supervision, while Hopfield networks, a special ANN with every node connected to every other node, act as associative memory and tend to converge based on similarities. **Boltzmann machines** (**BMs**) and **restricted Boltzmann machines** (**RBMs**) are variants of the Hopfield network that have additional restrictions and are trained using unsupervised learning approaches, making them great at extracting discriminative features from input data.

Recurrent neural networks

An RNN is a feed-forward network like what we've seen already. The significant difference is that they are not stateless. This means that rather than depending exclusively on the previous input, they also have a connection (arching lines on top of each perceptron in *Figure 3.9*) that feeds an input directly from their output.

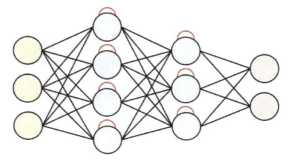

Figure 3.9: RNNs

The effect of this change is that the order of the input received by each node matters. So, if the network is analyzing the value of Bitcoin, it considers that a few months back, its value was around €60,000, whereas today, it went down to €20,000. If the temporal relationship is not considered, then the network won't be able to learn how to predict market movements. Even though RNNs are extremely powerful, they suffer from a significant setback normally referred to as the **vanishing gradient problem**. When such networks learn using backpropagation or similar techniques, the error is propagated backward through the network. However, at one point, the adjustment propagated back is so small that it becomes irrelevant, and the network stops learning. Unfortunately, this happens before the network learns to represent the underlying function!

Notwithstanding this limitation, RNNs are widely used in AI and have various applications, ranging from autocompletion of sentences to stock market predictions. They are used when the input data is normally a sequence, so the temporal order is extremely important.

Competitive networks

Competitive networks, such as Kohonen networks and self-organizing maps, are an interesting type of artificial neural network that can learn to classify inputs without requiring explicit supervision. These networks use a learning process called **competitive learning**, in which the neurons in the network compete with each other to become activated and respond to the input data. When an input is presented to the network, as shown in *Figure 3.10*, each neuron calculates its activation level based on the input, and the neuron with the highest activation level *wins*, thus becoming the output of the network.

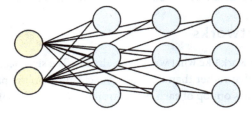

Figure 3.10: Competitive networks such as Kohonen networks and self-organizing maps

The winning neuron and its neighbors are then adjusted based on the input, with the winning neuron becoming more specialized in recognizing the particular input it won, and the neighboring neurons being adjusted to recognize similar inputs. This adjustment process further refines the network's classification abilities, making it particularly useful for applications where a large dataset is available, but the true classification labels are unknown or difficult to obtain. By learning to classify data in an unsupervised manner, competitive networks can help uncover hidden patterns and relationships in complex datasets. This makes them suitable for unsupervised learning tasks such as clustering and feature extraction.

Hopfield networks

A Hopfield network is a special ANN where every node is connected to every other node (as seen in *Figure 3.11*). What's interesting is the fact that the nodes have different uses. They serve as input nodes before the training starts; during the training, they act like the hidden layers, and after, they become the output nodes. When the network is trained on several patterns, it will always converge to one of the learned patterns since that guarantees the stability of the entire network. However, this does not work in all cases, and in most cases, only part of the network gains stability. Due to its particular structure, updating the network happens either synchronously or one at a time. Such networks are referred to as **associative memory** because they tend to converge based on the most common similarities. If this network is trained to identify faces, even though the image might have a lot of noise, it will still converge on one of the faces used for training since it is a property that emerges out of the interconnectedness of the ANN.

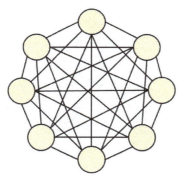

Figure 3.11: Hopfield network

A variant of the Hopfield network is the BM, whereby some neurons are labeled as input and others as hidden. At the end of the update, all the neurons of the full network become output neurons. The network is initially set up using random weights, which are subsequently adjusted using learning algorithms such as backpropagation (discussed earlier). The activation function is global and is controlled by a temperature value, meaning that it fires if it goes beyond a certain value (or temperature).

A further variation to BMs is the RBMs, as per *Figure 3.12*. They are, of course, built upon similar principles as the networks mentioned in this section; however, as the name implies, they have further restrictions. The main difference is that all the nodes are not connected to all the other nodes. However, the nodes are divided into groups (input and hidden), and each node in one group is connected to all the other nodes in the other group. This means that there is no interconnectedness between nodes forming part of the same group. RBMs are trained similarly to how we've seen before, but there's a significant difference. After the forward pass, the output is sent back to the first layer. Following that, forward-and-back propagation is used to train the network. Since RBMs utilize an unsupervised learning approach, they are extremely good at extracting discriminative features from input data.

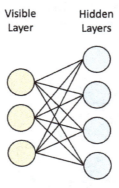

Figure 3.12: Restricted Boltzmann machine

So far, we've explained the fundamental workings of different ANN architectures. However, there are many more complex variants, and the previous section only provided an introduction. The next section will delve deeper into the workings of deep neural networks and explore these novel architectures. It will also give an overview of the advancements made in recent years.

Delving into deep neural networks

So far, we've scratched the surface of several ANNs, because there are so many variants that it would be very difficult to collate them all in this document, and it would be beyond the scope of this book. The main problem with ANNs was that toward the end of the last century, they hit a brick wall, and advancements were moving at a relatively slow pace.

This changed soon after the turn of the century due to three main reasons:

- The amount of information available online in digital form provided a fertile ground for data-hungry algorithms such as ANNs. Just consider that up to 90% of the world's data was created in the past 2 years, and is constantly increasing at an impressive rate of 2.5 quintillion bytes of data per day.

- The advancement in video game development. Back then, game developers were looking at ways in which they could improve the graphics. Because of this, they needed a more powerful and dedicated processor, which is how the **Graphics Processing Unit (GPU)** was born. The GPU is designed like a parallel computer capable of performing mathematical functions not just on one data item but on several at once. Coincidentally, this was precisely the kind of processing that was needed to process large and complex ANNs. Because of this, AI professionals started using GPUs, which proved to be a match made in heaven since this sped up the development of more complex models. Later, companies such as Google released their own specialized versions of the GPU specifically designed for AI applications, such as the **Tensor Processing Unit (TPU)**. During this period, we've also seen democratization in processing power thanks to the widespread availability of cloud processing. Thus, the combination of these factors led to the successful creation of more complex ANNs.

- The development and use of new ANNs architectures, normally referred to as **Deep Learning (DL)** approaches. Many of the underlying ideas are not entirely new, and some of them have been around for the past 70 years; however, their success was limited due to the issues mentioned earlier. DL is a class of algorithms that can be used to tackle a myriad of problems in very diverse domains.

In the coming section, we will be exploring various architectures used in DL. The word *deep* is normally attributed to the deep hidden layers found in these types of networks through which such networks derive their effectiveness in handling complex tasks. However, before delving into these architectures, it is important to note that these networks learn using several different approaches. The four main categories are as follows:

- **Supervised learning** occurs when the algorithm is provided with examples (normally input-output pairs), and the ANN learns to model that function.

- **Semi-supervised learning** uses a small subset of examples for learning. It then categorizes unseen examples and adds to the training set those examples that were labeled with high confidence. The process is repeated until all the items are eventually labeled.

- **Unsupervised learning** doesn't use any examples but tries to identify underlying patterns in the data to learn possible classifications.

- **Self-supervised learning** uses a semi-automatic process to learn to categorize from the data and then use that information to tackle the whole dataset.

Now that we have had a look at how DL algorithms learn, let's have a look at the most popular ones used in various applications.

Convolutional neural networks

A **convolutional neural network** (CNN) is a kind of network inspired by the biological evolution of the visual cortex. If we look at how the eye works, we find that various receptors specialize in recognizing different features such as colors, shapes, and so on. CNN works on similar principles, and because of this, it is very much adapted to tackle computer vision applications. Similarly, the network comprises various layers that perform visual extraction followed by classification, as seen in *Figure 3.13*. The input image is first divided into sections that feed into the convolutional layer.

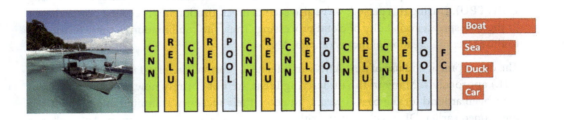

Figure 3.13: A CNN

These are used to extract features from that image. Of course, not all the features are important, so the **Rectified Linear Unit** (**ReLU**) is used as the activation function, which also helps to keep the gradient relatively constant while allowing the network to be trained without harmful consequences. The following step is **pooling**, which allows the CNN to focus on the most relevant patterns. It's a sort of lens that reduces the dimensionality of the features by informing us that a feature was present but not exactly where. By doing so, a small variation will not affect the final target while also managing memory and improving speed (especially in large images). There are various iterations of the architecture just described until, finally, all the output is passed through a **fully connected** (**FC**) multilayer perceptron at the end. This is where the classification happens. Such networks are normally trained using backpropagation and have been widely successful in applications related to image processing, video recognition, and several **Natural Language Processing** (**NLP**) tasks.

Long short-term memory networks

A **long short-term memory** (**LSTM**) network is a special kind of RNN that doesn't suffer from the vanishing gradient problem mentioned earlier. The basic architecture departs from the traditional neuron-based networks we've seen and uses a memory cell concept. The cell uses the memory component (as seen in *Figure 3.14*) to remember what's important for a short or longer period. It also contains three gates – input, forget, and output – which are used to control the flow of information within the network:

- The *input gate* regulates the flow of new information into memory

- The *forget gate* allows the network to dispose of existing information, thus making space for new data

- The *output gate* controls the usage of the data stored within each cell

LSTMs are extensively used in NLP applications since they are extremely good at processing sequences like the ones we use in natural languages. There are several variances of LSTMs, one of which is the **Gated Recurrent Unit** (**GRU**), which simplifies the existing LSTM model by removing the output gate. This makes the network use less memory and improves its performance; however, it tends to be less accurate than an LSTM when dealing with longer sequences.

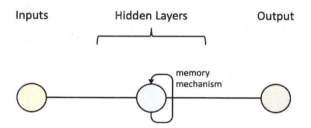

Figure 3.14: An LSTM architecture showing the memory mechanism,
which takes information from prior inputs

Autoencoders

An autoencoder (*Figure 3.15*) is a network of three layers; input, hidden, and output. However, unlike other networks, it gathers its input, encodes it in the hidden layer, and recreates it in the output layer.

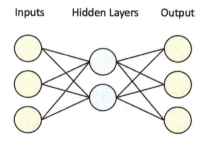

Figure 3.15: Autoencoder architecture

The hidden layer typically consists of fewer nodes than the input layer, and an encoding/decoding function is used to process the data. Because of this, the error is not calculated on the output only like most other networks but is a function that finds the difference between the input and output layer. The weights are then adjusted to reduce the error further. Also, since the autoencoders constantly encode and decode the same input, there is no need to compare the outputs with any additional data like in traditional techniques, thus making the network self-supervised. Such networks have been successfully used for image compression, denoising, and feature extraction.

Deep belief networks

A **deep belief network** (DBM) is a typical multilayer network with an input, several hidden layers, and an output. The main difference between this and typical multilayered architectures is in the training of such a network. Rather than performing a forward pass followed by backpropagation, each pair of layers (RBM$_1$, RBM$_2$, and RBM$_3$) is considered an individual RBM. Because of this, we can describe the DBM as a stack of RBMs, as can be seen in *Figure 3.16*.

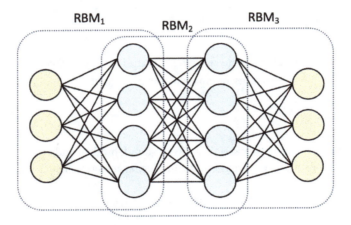

Figure 3.16: DBM architecture

The input layer gets a feed from the raw sensory input, and as the information passes through the hidden layers, it generates a different level of abstraction. The output layer then simply takes care of the final classification. The training is also divided into two phases: the first is the **unsupervised pretraining**, and the second is the **supervised fine-tuning**.

In the first phase, the second layer in every RBM is trained to reconstruct the first layer. So, the first hidden layer has to reconstruct the input layer. The second hidden layer must reconstruct the first hidden layer, and the output layer is trained to reconstruct the second hidden layer. Once all the layers have been pretrained, the second phase begins, whereby the output nodes are linked to labels to give them meaning. Once this is completed and all the weights are set, backpropagation (or any other training function) is used to finalize the training phase. Such networks have been used in sentiment analysis applications and personalization.

Generative networks

As the name implies, **generative networks** use DL methods such as CNNs (discussed earlier) to generate new information. The task comprises the automatic discovery and learning of patterns within the input data, which is then used to generate new plausible examples based on the original dataset.

The most popular ones are called **generative adversarial networks** (**GANs**), and they use a supervised learning approach. Rather than using one model, they have two: a *generator* and a *discriminator*. The role of the generator is to create new example data points based on the training dataset. These are then fed to the discriminator, which decides whether they exhibit the characteristics of the data found in the training set. If they don't, they are simply discarded, and a new example is created. This process continues until the discriminator model identifies new data with similar characteristics at least 50% of the time, thus indicating that the generator learned to replicate examples similar to the training data. Such an approach has been successfully used to generate new texts, paraphrase, and create artistic masterpieces.

Another important model gaining traction in recent years is the **diffusion model**. This model starts with a training set and gradually destroys it by inserting Gaussian noise, which is a statistical noise with a probability density equal to what one would expect in a normal distribution. The learner then tries to recover the data by removing the noise and replacing it with the correct value. After the training, the diffusion model can generate an image out of noisy data. This model has been extensively used in the creation of photo-realistic computer-generated images, as shown in *Figure 3.17*. It also has the benefit of not using any adversarial training (as in GANs) while being scalable and parallelizable.

Figure 3.17: Images generated using the Imagen diffusion model (source: imagen.research.google)

Transformers

A **transformer** is a machine learning model designed to process sequential data. However, it differs from traditional networks as it does not analyze the data sequentially but utilizes an attention mechanism that gives a higher weight to objects (such as words or images) based on their context.

Self-attention is a vital component of these transformer architectures since it identifies the most essential sections of a sequence. To do so, it does the following:

1. Encodes every object into a set of numbers (normally represented as a vector).

2. For every object and all the other words in the sentence, it calculates the product of the two vectors.

3. The results are normalized, multiplied by the existing weights, added together, and used as the new weights.

The effect of this process is that objects that have a semantic relationship are given more importance than others. As can be seen in *Figure 3.18*, the architecture uses a sequence-to-sequence model with a separate encoder and decoder.

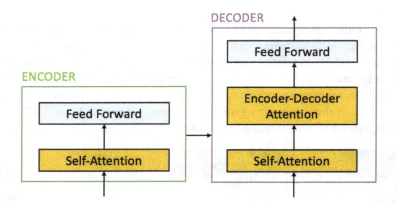

Figure 3.18: Typical transformer architecture

The encoder consists of blocks comprising the self-attention mechanism and the feed-forward network. The decoder has three blocks: the self-attention mechanism, an encoder-decoder attention component, and a feed-forward network. The main difference between the transformers and RNNs is that a transformer is not time-dependent; thus, objects are given importance based on the attention mechanism. Since their inception, transformers obtained massive popularity since their results almost reached a human level in various tasks, such as the following:

- **Text classification**: Assigning a label or category to a text, such as sentiment analysis, spam detection, and topic identification

- **Information extraction**: Extracting structured information from unstructured text, such as named entity recognition, relation extraction, and event extraction

- **Question answering (QA)**: Generating a natural language answer to a natural language question, such as reading comprehension, factoid QA, and open-domain QA

- **Summarization**: Producing a concise summary of a longer text or multiple texts, such as news articles, scientific papers, and reviews

- **Translation**: Converting a text from one language to another language, such as English to French, Chinese to English, and Hindi to Urdu

- **Text generation**: Creating new text based on some input or context, such as dialogue generation, story generation, and caption generation

Today, we live in the age of large language models with transformers such as GPT, BERT, T5, and many others integrated into several AI applications.

Comparing the networks

Let's now look at the pros, cons, and applications of the networks that we've discussed so far:

- **Artificial Neural Network**: Networks inspired by the structure and function of biological neurons:

  - **Pros**: Can learn complex patterns and relationships, and perform tasks such as classification, regression, and prediction

  - **Cons**: Can suffer from overfitting; may require a large amount of data and computing resources to train effectively

  - **Applications**: Image and speech recognition, natural language processing, and recommender systems

- **Recurrent Neural Networks**: Networks that can process sequences of inputs by passing information from one time step to the next:

  - **Pros**: Can model temporal dependencies and long-term dependencies; can handle variable-length inputs

  - **Cons**: Can suffer from vanishing and exploding gradients; can be computationally expensive to train

  - **Applications**: Natural language processing, speech recognition, and time series prediction

- **Competitive Networks**: Networks where neurons compete with each other for activation:

  - **Pros**: Can learn to classify inputs without explicit supervision; can identify prototypes or representatives in the data

- **Cons**: Limited to unsupervised learning; may require hand-crafted features
- **Applications**: Clustering and feature extraction

- **Hopfield Networks**: Networks that can store and retrieve memories as stable patterns of activation:

  - **Pros**: Can store a large number of memories; can tolerate noise and incomplete patterns
  - **Cons**: Limited to associative memory and pattern completion tasks; may converge to incorrect states or spurious memories
  - **Applications**: Pattern completion and optimization problems

- **Convolutional Neural Networks**: Networks that can learn hierarchical representations of inputs, particularly images:

  - **Pros**: Can learn spatial and translation-invariant features; can perform well with limited data
  - **Cons**: Can be computationally expensive to train; may require a large number of parameters
  - **Applications**: Image and video recognition, object detection, and segmentation

- **Long Short-Term Memory Networks**: Recurrent neural networks that can better handle long-term dependencies by selectively remembering or forgetting information:

  - **Pros**: Can model long-term dependencies and variable-length sequences; can handle noisy and incomplete inputs
  - **Cons**: Can be computationally expensive to train; may suffer from vanishing gradients
  - **Applications**: Natural language processing, speech recognition, and time series prediction

- **Autoencoders**: Networks that can learn compressed representations of inputs by encoding and decoding them:

  - **Pros**: Can learn meaningful representations of data; can perform data compression and denoising
  - **Cons**: Limited to unsupervised learning; may suffer from overfitting
  - **Applications**: Data compression, denoising, and feature extraction

- **Deep Belief Networks**: Networks composed of multiple layers of restricted Boltzmann machines, can learn hierarchical representations of data:

  - **Pros**: Can learn complex and abstract features; can perform unsupervised pretraining followed by supervised fine-tuning
  - **Cons**: Can be computationally expensive to train; limited to classification and generation tasks
  - **Applications**: Image and speech recognition and generative modeling

- **Generative Networks**: Networks that can generate new samples of data similar to the training data:

  - **Pros**: Can generate realistic and diverse samples; can be conditioned on specific inputs

  - **Cons**: Can be computationally expensive to train; may suffer from mode collapse

  - **Applications**: Image and speech synthesis, data augmentation, and anomaly detection

- **AI Transformers**: Networks that use self-attention mechanisms to process sequential data:

  - **Pros**: Can process sequential data of varying lengths; can capture long-range dependencies and achieve state-of-the-art performance in language modeling

  - **Cons**: Can be computationally expensive to train; may require large amounts of data for optimal performance

  - **Applications**: NLP, text generation, machine translation, speech recognition, and image captioning

In this section, we explored some of the most popular ANN architectures beyond the basic single-layer and multilayer perceptrons. Each architecture has its strengths and weaknesses, making it suitable for specific tasks. However, as we'll see in the next chapter, the rise of data has allowed researchers to train increasingly complex models that can handle more significant and complex datasets. The rise of big data has been a game-changer for machine learning, enabling researchers to develop new algorithms and techniques to tackle challenging problems. In the following chapter, we will delve deeper into the rise of data and its impact on the development of deep learning.

The rise of data

Data refers to the raw facts and figures that are collected and processed to provide useful information. In this context, data is essential for training models to recognize patterns and make predictions. The rise of data has been closely linked with the growth of the internet. As more people have come online and generated more information, the amount of data available has grown exponentially. This has had a profound impact on deep learning, enabling researchers to develop increasingly sophisticated models that can learn from vast amounts of data. As more people came online, companies began to realize the value of this data. They started collecting it en masse, using it to gain insights into customer behavior and preferences. This led to the emergence of big data – large datasets that were too complex to be processed using traditional methods. Big data presented a challenge for machine learning researchers. Traditional machine learning algorithms were not designed to handle such large amounts of information. However, this challenge also presented an opportunity to develop new algorithms that could learn from vast amounts of data.

One of the key technologies that have enabled this growth in data is the development of advanced sensors and devices. These devices can collect data on everything from temperature and humidity to heart rate and blood pressure. They can be embedded in everything from smartphones and wearable devices to cars and industrial machinery. As these devices have become more widespread, they have generated vast amounts of data. This data can be used to gain insights into everything from human behavior to machine performance. It has also enabled new applications such as predictive maintenance and personalized medicine. Big data has had a profound impact on many industries, including healthcare, finance, and retail:

- In healthcare, big data is being used to improve patient outcomes by analyzing large datasets to identify patterns and trends. For example, researchers can use big data to identify risk factors for diseases such as diabetes and heart disease.

- In finance, big data is being used to improve risk management by analyzing large datasets to identify patterns and trends. For example, banks can use big data to identify fraudulent transactions and assess credit risk.

- In retail, big data is being used to improve customer experiences by analyzing large datasets to understand customer behavior and preferences. For example, retailers can use big data to personalize marketing campaigns and improve inventory management. By analyzing customer purchase histories and browsing behavior, retailers can gain insights into what products are popular and when they are likely to sell out. This can help them optimize their inventory levels and reduce waste.

Overall, the internet and technology have enabled the creation and collection of massive amounts of data, which has had a profound impact on many industries, enabling new applications and improving efficiency. As technology continues to advance, it is likely that we will see even more innovative uses of big data in the future.

However, big data is not always available and, because of this, there is active research going on in the use of small data. This refers to datasets that are smaller in size and complexity compared to big data. Despite their smaller size, small datasets can still be incredibly valuable for deep learning. They can provide high-quality information that is relevant to a specific problem or domain. One of the key benefits of small data is that it can be easier to work with than big data. Small datasets are often more manageable and can be processed using traditional machine learning algorithms. This makes them a good choice for researchers who are just starting out in the field of deep learning.

In addition to small data, **synthetic data** is also becoming increasingly important in deep learning. It refers to artificially-generated data that is created using computer algorithms. This type of data can be used to augment existing small datasets or create entirely new ones. Another key benefit of synthetic data is that it allows researchers to generate large amounts of high-quality training data quickly and easily. This can be especially useful when working with complex problems such as image recognition or natural language processing.

To facilitate global research efforts, many datasets have been created, which played a key role in advancing deep learning research and applications. Some of the most widely used datasets include MNIST, MS-COCO, ImageNet, Open Images Dataset, VisualQA, and **Street View House Numbers (SVHN)**:

- **MNIST** is a dataset of handwritten digits that has become a benchmark for evaluating machine learning algorithms. It consists of 70,000 images of digits from 0 to 9. Each image is 28x28 pixels in size and is represented as a grayscale value.

- **MS-COCO** is a large-scale dataset for object detection, segmentation, and captioning. It contains over 330,000 images with more than 2.5 million object instances. The dataset includes a wide range of objects and scenes, making it a valuable resource for training deep learning models.

- **ImageNet** is another large-scale image dataset that has been widely used in deep learning research. It contains over 14 million images organized into more than 20,000 categories. The images in ImageNet are high-resolution and cover a wide range of subjects.

- The **Open Images Dataset** is another large-scale image dataset that has been used in deep learning research. It contains over 9 million images with diverse annotations such as object labels and bounding boxes.

- **VisualQA** is a dataset for visual question answering that contains over 250,000 images with associated questions and answers. The dataset is designed to test the ability of deep learning models to understand and reason about visual information.

- The **SVHN** dataset is a real-world image dataset for digit recognition. It contains over 600,000 images of house numbers extracted from Google Street View. The images are in color and vary in size and resolution.

These datasets have played a crucial role in advancing deep learning research and applications. They have provided researchers with large amounts of high-quality data that can be used to train and validate deep learning models. By using these datasets, researchers have been able to develop increasingly sophisticated models that can recognize patterns and make predictions with high accuracy.

In conclusion, data has played a crucial role in advancing deep learning research and applications. The rise of the internet and the development of advanced sensors and devices have enabled the creation and collection of massive amounts of data. This data has provided researchers with valuable resources for training and validating deep learning models. As a result, we have seen significant progress in many areas of deep learning research, including image recognition, natural language processing, and predictive analytics. Big data has also had a profound impact on many industries, including healthcare, finance, and retail. Overall, the rise of data has been a key driver of innovation in deep learning research and applications.

The complexities and limitations of neural networks

As we've seen in previous sections, ANNs are extremely powerful and extensively used in different AI applications. Notwithstanding this, they are very complex machines (some of them are reaching the one trillion parameter mark), and because of this, they suffer from various limitations. The following are some of the most critical issues.

The first issue with ANNs is their "black box" nature. When we refer to an algorithm, we mean that the algorithm can get a set of inputs and return a set of outputs, but we are not entirely sure about how it achieved those results since the inner workings are not visible. It's like looking at a black box machine, hence the name! So, if we create a neural network to distinguish between a cat and a dog, we cannot say how it managed to do it, whether it's the color of the animal, the pointy ears, or its long tail.

Human-interpretable features are much more preferred since, by analyzing them, we can have the certainty that the algorithm is not just working but also working well. Also, if there is a mistake, we can be in a better position to identify it and correct the origin of that mistake. Until ANNs become interpretable, it will be very hard to use them in critical situations, especially when people's lives are at stake.

In some applications, such as in the courts of justice, dishing out decisions about people's lives is not enough. Decisions must be justified, and those justifications need to follow coherent logic. If this information is not available, how is it possible for an accused person to ever defend themselves or appeal against the sentence? Because of this, *explainability* should be an inherent feature of many applications – something that ANNs still find hard to achieve.

The problem with infusing explainability within an ANN algorithm is related to complexity. Libraries such as Keras, PyTorch, and Caffe make the lives of programmers developing neural networks much more straightforward than if they had to program them from scratch. They do so by abstracting over mathematics, the details of the algorithm, and the hyperparameters. However, one shouldn't forget that even though these libraries are available, solving an AI problem is never easy. In most cases, very few people around the world would have solved a similar problem because AI is very pervasive and can be applied to almost anything. To tackle such a problem, one might have to resort to using lower-level libraries or maybe coding parts of the network from scratch. Of course, there is always a threshold between the coding complexity required and the improvement obtained. If the difference is not that much, it might be more worth opting for a simpler algorithm that might give you similar results.

Identifying the correct algorithm is only part of the story. ANNs typically make use of much more data than other traditional machine learning algorithms. Some of them even require labeled data, which might require human intervention. This tends to be very problematic because data is not always readily available, and when it is, the quality needs to be checked. In recent years, researchers have been moving away from the realms of big data and more toward creating better algorithms that can work with small data. When the data available is problematic, researchers are also looking at synthetic data, which allows them to generate massive amounts of data points in the lab.

Finally, once we have the algorithm and the data, we need to use them. This, unfortunately, tends to be computationally expensive, making it difficult for anyone to use large models on their personal computer. Training large networks can sometimes take several weeks to train from scratch. This is very different from what typically happens with traditional machine learning algorithms, which normally take a few hours or, at most, a few days.

So ANNs can be pretty challenging to use. Of course, this is the cost one needs to pay in exchange for all the power. However, research is also advancing at a very fast pace. In the coming years, we will see the development of better, more powerful models, which are explainable and within reach of everyone.

Summary

In this chapter, we looked at ANNs and how they evolved from simple concepts to powerful AI models. We also had a run-through of the most popular architectures in use today, starting from the humble perceptron and finishing with the powerful transformer model. Finally, we skimmed through the complexities and limitations of ANNs to get an overview of the open challenges that still exist – hence why we need to seek new, more powerful alternatives. Because of this, in our next chapter, we will look at explainable AI and its various approaches that help to build trust in AI systems.

4
The Need for Explainable AI

In the past few years, **artificial intelligence (AI)** has achieved impressive feats, much more than it ever did in the preceding decades. If we consider what happened in the last pandemic, AI was instrumental in helping the pharmaceutical industry develop a vaccine in record time. But AI's extensive use is widespread in detecting all sorts of cancers, developing new drugs, and rehabilitating patients. On another front, we now have self-driving cars taking us from one place to the other, our airplanes are flown by an auto-pilot 90% of the time, and the level of safety we've reached is unheard of. If we look at basic human tasks, the ImageNet competition showed that even when it comes to simply labeling images (something we learned to do when we were still infants), an AI is capable of achieving much more accurate results. The list of examples can keep on going forever since AI systems can be found in most applications. The truth is that AI can augment itself to most human functions. It's not only enhancing our throughput but also, in some cases, achieving results that are way better than what any human alone can ever attain.

No one can deny that the results obtained in various disciplines are impressive. However, we must be careful. The democratization of AI also means that anyone can download a machine learning model and use it in their applications. While there's nothing wrong with that, you must be extremely careful that the proper scientific process is followed. Otherwise, as the IBM programmer George Fuechsel once said, "*Garbage in, garbage out!*"

The democratization of AI can be compared to a teenager learning to drive a car. The practice session is held in a confined environment without too many obstacles. This is done to prevent the young driver from causing potential damage. The young driver is always followed by an instructor who suggests minor improvements as they go along. When the instructor is satisfied with the level of driving achieved by the young apprentice, the instructor then increases the difficulty level by first driving on secondary roads and then on main roads. When it comes to AI, someone who is capable of switching on the car thinks that they can drive perfectly well on the main road. Many programmers are not mentored by an AI expert – they download one of the many freely available models, train it, and if it returns an accuracy close to 100%, then it is deemed successful.

But the truth is very far from that – high accuracy is not necessarily an indication of a successful model. The most common reason for high values is overfitting. This means that the model did not manage to generalize, and because of this, it fits the training data exactly. Imagine that we have the task of distinguishing between pictures of cats and dogs. The problem here is that while such a model is extremely good at classifying the pictures found in the training set if it is shown a new picture of an unseen dog, it is incapable of classifying it correctly. Of course, this is just one of the potential problems and there might be many others. Because of this, basing our success simply on accuracy levels might be misleading. We need an AI capable of giving us a justification for how it reached a particular conclusion, which is why we need **explainable artificial intelligence (XAI)**.

XAI is a set of techniques designed to help human users comprehend and trust the results obtained by AI algorithms. It is used to describe an AI model (particularly those that are complex, such as deep learning algorithms), and its expected impact gives the results and shows any potential biases. By doing so, it reinforces the validity of the results while auditing the fairness, accentuating transparency, and reassuring the users that the results can be trusted for decision-making processes.

In the following sections, we'll have a look at various aspects of XAI so that we can understand why it is needed. We will do so by looking at the potential dangers of using machine learning models without proper scientific processes. This chapter will focus on the need for XAI techniques, which help users comprehend and trust the results obtained by AI algorithms.

The overall goal of this chapter is to explain the importance of XAI and how it reinforces the validity of results while auditing fairness, increasing transparency, and reassuring users that results can be trusted for decision-making processes. This information is important because it highlights the potential risks of relying solely on high accuracy levels without considering the generalization of models, and it emphasizes the need for XAI techniques to ensure the validity and reliability of AI-generated results.

Specifically, we will cover the following topics in this chapter:

- What is XAI?
- Why do we need XAI?
- The state-of-the-art models in XAI

What is XAI?

XAI is a recent field of study that deals with designing AI models that are easier to understand. The need for such a field arose from the fact that, in recent years, there has been a move toward statistical AI since the results obtained from such a system were incredible, not only on a par with humans in most instances but also reaching super-human levels in various applications. Unfortunately, since statistical approaches use probabilities, even though superior, the resulting model is rather hard to read. As such, it is difficult to interpret its correctness in all cases.

For example, if tasked with creating a loan application system, we might devise a set of rules similar to those displayed in *Figure 4.1*:

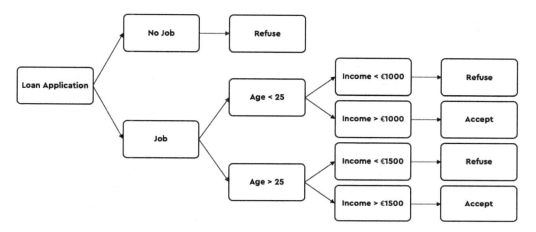

Figure 4.1: Rule-based loan application process

These rules are easy to understand, even for someone who is not computer literate. These are usually called rule-based systems, which fall under the symbolic AI paradigms. However, when the process starts to become complex, it might be hard to develop these rules. Sometimes, it would be impossible to handcraft them one by one. Because of this, AI scientists resort to statistical AI. They gather a bunch of historic data, process it, and generate an automated set of rules, similar to those in *Figure 4.2*. As can be seen from the diagram, the rules are practically the same, even though they might be more accurate. However, they are much more challenging to understand with the naked eye, if not impossible!

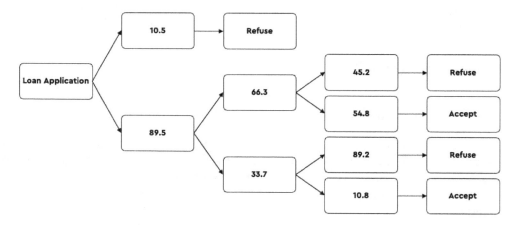

Figure 4.2: Statistical-based loan application process

Of course, this diagram only shows a toy example to explain the concept. But imagine one of the big language models having a network of around 1 trillion parameters. How can a human being ever think of understanding what's happening? It's simply impossible. We refer to these AI systems as a **black box model**.

Think about it as a sausage machine. Insert some input from the left, let it process it, and get some output from the right. However, since it's a black box, we cannot look into it and are not privy to the internal workings of the algorithm. The opposite of a black box is a **glass box**. It works in precisely the same way, but since the outer shell is made of glass, we can peep into its workings and see precisely what's happening inside. A glass box process is explainable by design and therefore does not need XAI. So, to recap, rule-based systems like the one in *Figure 4.1* are glass boxes, and statistical ones like those in *Figure 4.2* are like black boxes.

XAI deals with finding ways of making black boxes less opaque. This is achieved using various approaches. XAI algorithms might look at the properties of the model and try to interpret them by giving meanings to the different components (such as the neurons or the attribute changes). They might also try to create an understandable representation of the internal logic behind a single decision or even try to describe all the internal workings of the system. Some of these algorithms do so by generating instructions using a rule-based approach. Others generate input-output pairs to denote the internal workings of the system using a case-based exploratory approach. Then, it's up to the user to infer logic from such pairs. Considering the previous example of annotating images of cats and dogs, a rule-based approach would create a set of generic rules to distinguish between the two types of animals. On the other hand, the case-based approach would gather pictures that match the input requirements and present those.

Unfortunately, creating glass boxes is not so straightforward. An expert can create hand-crafted rules, but this is a rather difficult task that becomes somewhat impossible when dealing with complex systems. Rule-based, case-based, and other approaches do not always produce good results, hence why there is a drive for a new breed of algorithms such as neuro-symbolic AI, which will be discussed in the next chapter.

Why do we need XAI?

We have seen various technical reasons why we need XAI. All of them are very valid and extremely important. However, there are others that we should consider:

- **Human readability**: Since AI permeates every aspect of our society, it is not surprising that it is extensively used for decision-making. However, our world is becoming increasingly more complex. With the rise in **Internet of Things** (**IoT**) devices, where everything is connected to the internet, we are in a position to measure everything much more accurately than was practically possible a few years back. Of course, this raises a new problem: all the data that's harvested cannot be physically processed manually. It's simply impossible. The only practical solution we have is to use AI systems capable of crunching vast volumes of numbers in an incredibly short amount of time. Thus, our reliance on AI is steadily increasing. Directors or **Chief Executive Officers (CEOs)** of various companies need to collate the suggestions provided by the AI and make informed decisions. They need to trust the AI and assume that the results are correct. XAI comes to the rescue because it gives the reasoning behind certain decisions that might appear opaque. Doing so will also increase transparency since the various components of a decision are explained and can be scrutinized. Such an approach gives decision-makers the peace of mind to better understand automated business decisions.

- **Justifiability**: Every decision needs to be justified. This is not just a good practice that can be used to increase transparency and eventually trust but is also a moral right. If a person is affected in some way by a decision made by someone else, they need to understand why that decision was taken on their behalf. Not just that, but the onus of certain decisions is placed on the people who take them.

  If we consider the **General Data Protection Regulation (GDPR)** that has been in force in the European Union since 2018, it specifically requests the data collector to have valid reasons for gathering data – they have to collect only what they need and nothing more. Furthermore, after using the data, they must delete it. Failure to abide by this regulation might lead to serious legal consequences. There have been various cases where companies made decisions without adequately informing their employees and clients. By doing so, they exposed themselves to legal action, and some got sued. Thus, if a machine suggests a particular course of action and the decision maker is unaware of the justifications, they can be liable to risk.

- **Discrimination**: In today's world, any form of discrimination is unacceptable. We are all equals, and everyone should enjoy the same rights, irrespective of their differences. It is unfortunate that inequalities still exist and stereotypes prevail. This can easily be tested by going on Google and searching for images of doctors and nurses. The prevailing number of doctor images show male doctors; the opposite happens for nurses. In itself, this reflects the gender disparities that exist in our world. But the problem arises when this publicly available data is fed to an AI. Intelligent systems do not make distinctions between one gender or another – for them, they're just numeric representations. Thus, if you were to train an AI on that data, the imbalance in the training dataset will automatically result in discrimination.

  This is precisely what happened with Amazon. The multinational e-commerce company employs more than 1.5 million people globally. So, you can imagine the scale of recruitment that they adopt. To streamline this process, Amazon engineers came up with the idea of creating an AI capable of sifting through the applications and shortlisting the most promising candidates, thus helping **human resources (HR)** save time. Like most AI systems, they needed data for training, so they thought of using the **curricula vitae (CVs)** of people who already work for Amazon. Their reasoning was relatively sound. If someone passed through the selection process and already worked for Amazon, the new candidates should have similar attributes. The system was eventually trained and produced a good enough accuracy to be used on real candidates. However, the HR personnel noticed something strange in the results: the system was consistently preferring male candidates and rejecting female applicants. On deeper inspection, the engineers realized that the fault was with the data. In large tech companies such as Amazon, only around one-fourth of employees are female. So, when using the CVs of existing employees, engineers inadvertently introduced a bias in the system that discriminated against female candidates. Even though this discrimination was unintentional, using a black box algorithm makes it difficult to uncover such issues until it is too late.

- **Improvements**: The world we live in is very dynamic; things are constantly changing and, as such, we have to respond to those changes swiftly. One of the biggest problems with automated systems is that when they work well, people tend to forget about them and only remember that they exist when things go astray. This is precisely what happened in Malta when they installed a speed camera on the sidewalk next to a landscaped area. The camera worked perfectly, fatalities decreased from the stretch of road, and it was returning a healthy income stream. Many years passed, and everyone forgot about it because the objective was met. One day, a government official noticed that one of the trees in the landscaped area had grown so much that it was obfuscating the camera's view. When they checked, it was obvious the camera was not working, it generated no income, and fatalities increased again. Just because a system is working doesn't mean that it is working well. As the world changes, improving the system gets even more complex if the internal working of the AI is hidden from the engineers that should be maintaining it. In the case of the speed camera, the maintenance people might have realized something was different but didn't realize it was due to the tree in front of the camera. With a lack of information, they might have thought that it was due to better driving, less traffic, or a million other possible reasons. Unfortunately, we all know that *correlation does not necessarily imply causation*. But without all the information, it is difficult to understand what's happening.

- **Overfitting**: Many AI systems obtain impressive results, but some are too good to be true. When training such systems, you have to be extra careful about the possibility that the algorithm learned the training data so well that it can only recognize those examples and nothing else. This is usually called overfitting because the algorithm perfectly memorized the training data. A good indication of overfitting is when the algorithm's precision hovers around 99%. While this might sound great, in reality, it only means that the system did not manage to reach generalization. Let's look at a simple example.

If we're tasked with creating a classifier to identify between images of cats and dogs, and we use four images as test data (two from each category), we are confident that the AI will distinguish between the two categories with 100% accuracy. While such a result might sound fantastic, as soon as we provide it with a fifth image that it has never seen before, the system will fail miserably. This is because the algorithm did not generalize the features of the two categories beyond the test data but only learned to distinguish between those four images. When creating such a system, we will never have the images of all the cats and dogs that exist. Thus, this poses a problem, and because of this, we need algorithms capable of generalizing beyond the test data.

Black box AI does not manage to identify the right relationships, and if we cannot understand which connections were picked, then we cannot find ways of improving the system. We need systems that we can understand so that we can be sure that the AI algorithm is looking at the bigger picture and not at a subset of it, hence why we need XAI!

XAI case studies

To better understand the importance of XAI, it is important to contextualize it in several real-world applications. It is crucial to realize that an AI system that does not produce good results is not just a technical issue but can have real consequences on people's lives. Let's look at some cases.

Classification

A few years back, the University of Washington embarked on a rather challenging classification task, that of identifying between Huskies and wolves. Although it might seem simple initially, on further inspection, the undertaking becomes rather tricky due to the impressive similarities between the two animals.

They obtained several images representing the two animals in different contexts and used those to train a classifier. In line with AI best practices to avoid overfitting, the system was also tested on an independent set of unseen images, which is usually the case. Surprisingly, even though distinguishing between the two animals is very difficult for humans, the AI achieved an astonishing 90% accuracy. Of course, the researchers were very happy with such a result, but they wanted to understand how the AI manages such a feat. It could be that it managed to detect features that humans missed or some attributes that were underestimated. However, when they ran an explainer function to provide the reasons behind the AI's classification, it was immediately evident that the system based its judgment on the image's background. On analyzing hundreds of photos, the AI learned that wolf images were taken in the wild and usually had a snowy background.

On the other hand, Huskies, being domesticated animals, were usually portrayed in a more urban setting. Rather than creating a wolves versus Huskies classifier, unwittingly, all they made was a complex snow detector. The lesson from this is that just by looking at the performance of such systems, we would not be able to catch such faults.

Medical

When faced with a growing workload, many organizations resort to automation to relieve some of the pressures assaulting their workforce. This is what happened in Pittsburgh around the early 1990s. Since the local hospital was overwhelmed with an increasing number of pneumonia cases, they decided to conduct a study to predict the risks of complications in patients. The idea was to create a system that would categorize patients into two groups, low and high risk. Those in the low-risk category were sent home with a cocktail of antibiotics and ordered to rest. The others were admitted to the hospital immediately. In so doing, they would relieve the stress on the doctors and allow them to focus on the most complicated and life-threatening cases. The programmers decided to create an **Artificial Neural Network (ANN)**, which would analyze historic data amounting to around three-quarters of a million medical records obtained from the 78 hospitals participating in the study. The records were very representative of what was happening on the ground, and they even documented an 11% death rate. On training the system using this data, they obtained an 86% precision, which is an acceptable measure for such systems.

However, when the doctors tested the system with actual patients, they noticed a problem. When asthmatic patients with pneumonia were inputted into the system, the AI classified them as low risk. Any medical professional knows that someone with asthma is susceptible to lung infections, so there must be something wrong with the system. Thus, they raised red flags and stopped using the AI until further investigations were conducted by the programming team.

The programmers returned to the drawing board and analyzed every aspect of the system, but they could not find anything suspicious about how it was behaving. They also checked the data that was used for training, but still, everything seemed in line. They did all they could, but they hit a brick wall because they couldn't look into the inner workings of the AI. The ANN was a black box system, so extracting an explanation from it was somewhat complicated and, in some cases, even impossible. As a workaround for this hurdle, they decided to use a rule-based system, which is not as good as an ANN, but at least they could analyze the internal workings of the system. The new system generated all the rules and finally managed to go through them, but to their horror, the rule-based system also generated a rule that said that if the person is asthmatic and has pneumonia, they should be considered low risk.

This was indeed a mystery worthy of a seasoned investigator. On further investigation, the researchers understood what was happening. In the historic data they were using, they had the original symptoms and the outcomes but were missing the therapy used. Thus, it transpired that asthmatic patients with pneumonia did have a higher rate of recovery than the others (as correctly identified by the algorithm), but this was because they were given better quality care. They were immediately admitted to intensive care, and as a result, they managed to recover. So, even though there was nothing wrong with the algorithms and the data used, the fact that crucial information was missing made all the difference. This goes to show two important things – the first is that correlation does not imply causation, and the second is that human intuition is extremely important. If it weren't for the doctors, many more patients would have died that year!

Recruiting

We have already seen recruitment fail at Amazon. However, this is not an isolated case. Various companies are going down the same route. While Amazon is well known, so this news might sound sensational, how many more companies exist that are doing the same, if not worse, and we're not privy to their deeds? Furthermore, let's not forget that these new algorithms not only analyze the content on the CV of the candidate but they also snoop around on their social media accounts. Since most of our lives are exposed online, how fair is it to prevent potential candidates from getting their dream job or promotion simply because traces of past mistakes still linger online? Worse still, let's not forget that AI systems are not infallible, and while surfing online, they might quickly gather information about someone with a similar name. Cases of mistaken identities are numerous and constantly increasing. Recruiters have to be extremely cautious because their decisions must be transparent and legally defensible, something that is very difficult to achieve with a black box AI. This issue is further accentuated in regulated industries such as financial services, where they cannot afford any bias in their selection algorithms; otherwise, they will expose themselves to discrimination lawsuits and other legal nightmares.

Criminal sentencing

A juridical conviction can break a person forever, and this is even worse when a miscarriage of justice occurs. This was the case of Robert Williams, a family man who was spending some quality time with his daughters during a cold winter day in Detroit. Suddenly, the neighborhood lit up with the flashing lights of police cars approaching, and the children's laughter was suffocated by the wailing of their sirens. In a fraction of a second, which was too short to mentally process, Mr. Williams was apprehended and taken away amid the cries of his family. Transparency was thrown out of the window that day; no one bothered to explain what happened, and he was detained for 30 long hours in police custody. Subsequently, he was arraigned for theft and released with a $1,000 bond.

Mr. Williams understood that he was being charged with theft from a local jewelry store. The AI had matched his face with that of one of the robbers, hence why the charges were issued. There was no turning back now; he had to prove his innocence. Luckily for him, at the time of the robbery, he published a post on social media that proved that he was somewhere else. But the story could have taken a very negative twist. The police's over-reliance on AI led to this false arrest. The facial recognition software identified Mr. Williams from a database of 49 million images. However, the police failed to realize that even the most advanced computer vision algorithms have a 5% error, and Mr. Williams fell into that category.

But not everyone is so lucky. A Wisconsin man was sentenced to 6 years in jail by another system called Compass. The AI analyzed all the variables, and the result was that he was tagged as a threat to his community. The problem with this analysis is that since the algorithm is proprietary to a private organization, they are not bound to disclose how the AI works and why certain decisions were taken. A post-judgment analysis of the system quickly uncovered that statistically, white defendants were more likely to be incorrectly judged with a higher recidivism rate.

In China, they have an even more complex system known as the social score. A network of around 200 million public cameras and an army of sensors is constantly gathering information about the country's citizens to reward or punish people who don't exhibit trustworthy behavior. In some districts, they took it further by using advanced predictive analytics to prevent crime before it happens. So, if I'm an individual well known for forced entry into luxury apartments and I happen to pass through a high-end district, the police will monitor my movements and apprehend me if I exhibit any suspicious behavior.

It is clear from these examples that AI is already being used to make profound life-changing decisions. While the intention is probably good, we must remember that no system is infallible and that human intuition should also factor as part of the equation. Because of this, using glass boxes when making decisions that will impact humans' lives is imperative.

Autonomous vehicles

Self-driving vehicles are also not privy to controversies. Even though they might be orders of magnitude safer than human-operated machines, people are still skeptical when trusting their lives to the hand of AI. There is still a trust issue, which will take time until it is surpassed. This is ironic, considering that in modern aviation, almost 90% of the flight is entrusted to AI. Furthermore, recent innovations have also developed systems capable of handling the remaining 10%. But people need the reassurance that even if AI is in control, there's a person behind it ready to take over when things go wrong.

The challenge with cars is much more significant. In the aviation industry, we have around 25,000 planes worldwide, and they operate in a highly regulated environment with safety features in place. The automobile industry has around 1.4 billion vehicles worldwide operating in diverse environments with less stringent regulations and safety features. Because of this, self-driving cars must be able to reassure their users.

We've already experienced various accidents by high-profile companies whereby the autonomous vehicle bashed into a stationary obstacle, killing some of the passengers. Once again, there was no visibility on the cause of the accident, and these accidents were concealed. Of course, this does not help increase the trust users have in the system. Furthermore, there have been various studies that were rather worrying.

A recent study by researchers at the Georgia Institute of Technology found that some of the widely used computer vision algorithms (typically found in self-driving cars) find it difficult to detect people with darker skin tones, thus placing them at a higher risk of collision. Once again, the problem boils down to bias inside the AI. This was also confirmed by another study conducted by Google researchers, whereby their AI system completely missed people with a dark skin color.

In another instance, Tencent's Keen Security Lab shows how they can trick a self-driving car by placing three small stickers on the road. Even though they're tiny, the sophisticated sensors installed on the self-driving cars manage to detect them, and the AI interprets them as signifying a left veering lane, thus steering the car into a wall.

Of course, these failures are somewhat normal when testing new technologies. Hence, it is crucial to conduct them in a controlled environment to ensure that no one gets hurt. However, we also need to understand how AI algorithms make their decisions because if we don't, these hacks will keep disrupting the mass deployment of autonomous vehicles.

Military applications

It is no surprise that various countries are conducting active research on using AI for military purposes. In recent wars, we've seen various use cases where AI has been extensively used, such as the following:

- The identification of victims using biometrics
- The location of persons of interest via satellite tracking
- The snooping of enemy communication channels using natural language processing technologies
- The deployment of drone surveillance in sensitive areas
- The use of autonomous weapons capable of detecting and destroying enemy targets
- The development of humanoid robots aimed at replacing foot soldiers on the battlefield one day

Billions of dollars are being pumped yearly to create more sophisticated AI military applications. However, even though novel technologies are being developed at a quick pace, the US Department of Defense flagged explainability as a significant stumbling block, so much so that the **Defense Advanced Research Projects Agency (DARPA)** launched an XAI program to overcome these hurdles. Through this program, analysts are using AI to identify patterns in surveillance data and come up with human-understandable explanations. This is important for a variety of reasons. First, all decisions taken on the battlefield need to be transparent and accountable. Any "justified" harm to human life during a war cannot be left to the discretion of the few but must withstand scrutiny by the higher powers in office. Second, if autonomous vehicles keep increasing, it is only fair that they are tried and tested well before any military personnel can entrust their life. Thus, to safeguard the lives of their soldiers, analysts are reluctant to act on information without a clear explanation.

Time to explain

After seeing these case studies, it is evident that we need to move toward XAI. We cannot rely only on the correctness of current AI models since they are opaque, non-intuitive, and complex for people to understand. If we want people to trust autonomous decisions taken by these systems, users must understand how to manage the AI effectively. Let's not forget that algorithms and automation are becoming more pervasive. It permeates every aspect of our life. Businesses are heavily relying on AI-driven analytics, and we've started to see inroads in domains where the human expert was traditionally uncontested (for example, the judiciary, medical diagnostics, and so on). AI has several benefits over its human counterparts since it's precise, faster, doesn't get tired or sick, and will not go on holiday. However, as we've seen in the previous examples, biases and erroneous decisions can spread quickly.

Today, we are facing a situation where AI models are becoming more significant with millions of parameters, thus making them impossible to understand by humans. Some of these models offer little control over the underlying logic, and there are no simple means of correcting any errors that might arise.

With the introduction of the European GDPR, black box approaches have become much more challenging to use in business since they cannot explain their internal workings. Two fundamental rights enshrined in the law are the right to erasure and the right to be forgotten. This means that technically, anyone can make a request to any institution and demand the erasure of their private data. However, when the data is stored within an AI model, the situation becomes much more complex than it sounds because it is not just a matter of removing someone's data from a file. It has to be deleted from the database storing that data, from crash recovery backups, from data mirrored in data centers, and physically deleted from the hard disk (rather than just removing the link). This makes the erasure task extremely complex.

Given all these challenges, we need to find ways of making AI models explainable, and in the following section, we will look at some of the most prominent techniques currently in use.

The state-of-the-art models in XAI

XAI is a research area that has been gaining popularity in the past few years. In this section, we will look at a synthesis of the most critical XAI models in use today.

Accumulated Local Effects

The **Accumulated Local Effects** (ALE) method computes the effects of features globally. It is mainly used with tabular data, where different variables can be compared. The idea behind ALE is that if we have a small enough window, we can create an accurate estimate of the changes within a specific period. So, if we have a variable and we can sample its values across different periods, we can create an accurate estimate of how that variable is changing over time. The process is then repeated across all the accumulated data and is used to augment the global prediction. The algorithm focuses on the changes between one sampling point and the other, thus making the data relatively easy to interpret for any analyst.

Anchors

Anchors try to explain the behavior of complex models using high-precision rules. These rules define the local conditions using if-then statements, which ensure a prediction with high confidence. The focus is shifted to the input, which is essential for the classifier to make its predictions. Because of this, anchors are relatively easy to understand and apply to any data, thus making them model-agnostic. The assumption anchors use is that even though the model might be too complex globally, it can be explained by zooming into individual predictions. As can be seen in *Figure 4.3*, the anchor of the image identifies the dog. Thus, we can be sure that the AI is working correctly since no additional anchors are referenced by the AI. This contrasts significantly with the wolf versus Huskies case study we discussed earlier since, in that case, the anchor was referencing the snow and not the animal.

Figure 4.3: Photo of a dog on the left and its anchor on the right

Contrastive Explanation Method

The **Contrastive Explanation Method** (**CEM**) creates local explanations based upon particular instances. It defines **Pertinent Positives** (**PPs**) and **Pertinent Negatives** (**PNs**). Essentially, the PP finds the essential features of a data item to categorize that element as part of the positive examples. PN is the opposite and identifies the components without which the classification should maintain the same output. So, if we want to recognize the number 1, we can quickly identify the PP and PN:

$$1 \quad 1 \quad 1 \quad 1 \quad 1 \quad 1 \quad 1 \quad 1 \quad 1 \quad 1$$

Figure 4.4: Varied designs for the number 1

As we can see from these 10 examples of the various designs for the number 1, the long line that makes the number from top to bottom will be considered a PP since it is an essential element of all the different variants of the written number 1. However, any other additional horizontal or diagonal line used in the different styles is superfluous and would be considered a PN. Because of this, CEM is designed to be applied locally.

Counterfactual instances

Counterfactual explanations is a model-agnostic XAI technique that checks the AI model using explanations that describe the slightest change in a feature that would eventually change the prediction. These rules take the form of, "*If X had not occurred, Y would not have occurred.*"

The first part of the statement defines the event, while the second part is the causation. The model looks at the edge examples and notes what would happen. So, if we consider the example of taking a bank loan, a change in salary is an event that would allow the person to take a higher loan. Of course, not all the counterfactual instances are doable. While a change in salary might be possible (due to a pay rise, promotion, extra jobs, and so on), if we consider the motive behind rental property prices, the location is a significant factor but not something we can change. Since counterfactual instances deal with granular data, they are applied locally.

Explainable Boosting Machine

An **Explainable Boosting Machine** (**EBM**) is an interpretable model that uses machine learning techniques such as bagging and gradient boosting over traditional **Generalized Additive Models** (**GAMs**). A GAM is a linear model that also allows complex non-linear features. EBM works by building trees and performing a cyclic gradient-boosting GAM with interaction detection. This results in models that are typically highly accurate and comparable to state-of-the-art black boxes but with the benefit of also being completely interpretable. They are also very compact and fast. The downside is that EBMs usually take longer to train than other comparing algorithms. Due to their nature, they can be used for both local and global predictions.

Global Interpretation via Recursive Partitioning

Global Interpretation via Recursive Partitioning (**GIRP**) creates a binary tree representing a global machine learning model. The most vital rules, which are selected using a contribution matrix (obtained from the input variables), are represented as branches in the binary tree. To generate such a tree, a recursive process is launched, which partitions the input variables based on their contribution to the search space. Since it is applied to the global model, it cannot give local explanations like the other models.

Integrated gradients

Integrated gradients also work with input features of an AI model and assign them different importance levels based on the change in gradient. The gradient is gradually changed, and at every iteration, the effect of the different input features is noted. In doing so, we can identify which are essential and which aren't, thus allowing us to zoom in and focus on the most promising features. Such a technique is model-agnostic and can be used to explain any kind of data. This technique is rather popular and has been used not only to understand feature importance but also to identify skewed data and debug AI performance. Integrated gradients are typically applied locally.

Local interpretable model-agnostic explanations

As the name implies, **local interpretable model-agnostic explanations** (LIME) is both model-agnostic and focuses on local interpretations. When presented with a model and a test sample, LIME uses the data found in the test samples to create new synthetic data that follows a normal distribution. This new data is then fed to the existing model and used to generate new predictions. Each feature set is then weighted by checking the quality of the results vis-à-vis the original data points.

In so doing, the most critical features are selected. The most remarkable mechanism of the model is that it creates a sort of glass box surrounding the black box algorithm. As can be seen in *Figure 4.5*, in the case of the wolves versus Huskies case study, the background of the image was more important for the classification of the animal than the actual features of the wolves:

Figure 4.5: Image with recognized features marked using a red tint
(adapted from source: Madeleine Lewander from Pixabay)

Morris Sensitivity Analysis

Morris Sensitivity Analysis (MSA) implements a **one-step-at-a-time** (OAT) approach that analyzes the sensitivity of the global model. At any point, only one input has its level adjusted during every run. Such an approach is usually much faster than similar models. However, it might risk missing non-linearities. Such a model is usually used to determine which input is more critical for additional analysis, and it can only be applied globally.

Partial dependence plot

A **partial dependence plot** (**PDP**) shows the effect of various features on the predicted outcome. It can provide insight into the relationships between a feature and a target. These can form a linear, monotonic, or complex relationship. In a linear relationship, variables change similarly and at the same rate. A monotonic relationship is similar because variables change similarly but at a different rate. Even though PDP can be relatively quick at providing explanations, it assumes feature independence. However, we all know this condition is not always true and can be misleading if not met. Such a model typically works on the global model.

Permutation importance

Permutation importance measures the input feature's significance based on the increase in the model's error. The underlying assumption is that the model's error should also change if we shuffle the values of the pattern. Suppose the change in values does not affect the global error level. In that case, it simply means that the feature is probably unimportant since, irrespective of its value, it has almost no effect on the final output. On the other hand, if a change in the permutations drastically affects the output error, then there is a strong link, and the feature cannot be ignored when devising an explanation for that model. To identify these features, one of them is removed from the dataset, the estimator is re-trained, and the score is checked. Since we're working on the whole model, permutation importance only works at a global level.

Protodash

Protodash presents a novel approach based on the premise that a few representative prototypes can represent the most critical data points. This concept is interesting because, in the past few years, we've seen a surge in the creation of enormous language models such as GPT3, BERT, and many others. However, many people question whether the models' size can be reduced and still obtain comparative results. Varying research seems to suggest that this is possible since a big chunk of what's in the model appears redundant in most cases. Protodash does just that by weighing each prototype to evaluate its representation level of data.

The system requires three essential inputs: the dataset that needs explaining, the collection from where to extract the prototypes, and the number of prototypes to choose from. Protodash will identify different prototypes, thus seeking a more comprehensive representation of the underlying data. When a prototype is found, the next prototype that's sought will also model the underlying data but will have new characteristics different from the other prototype. By using this approach, the system guarantees a broader representation. The prototype search continues until the number of prototypes (defined a priori) is reached. Since the system finds targeted prototypes, it provides local results.

SHapley Additive exPlanations

SHapley Additive exPlanations (SHAP) is a framework that uses Shapley values to explain the output of a model. These values are often used in game-theoretic approaches to average the expected marginal contribution of a player after all the different combinations are considered. They determine a payoff for players based on their contributions. The idea is that an outcome can be explained based on the proportions of the input feature set. Because of this, the model can be applied both locally and globally.

Summary

In this chapter, we looked at XAI to understand what it is and why it is so important, especially within the context of black-box AI models. We also saw how, due to the increasing complexity of these models, XAI is somewhat inevitable. Following that, we also looked at various case studies, some of which were rather eye-opening, especially when considering that AI is being augmented in every aspect of our lives. Finally, we presented a non-exhaustive list of XAI methodologies. The models shown were the most popular and representative of various novel approaches in the field of XAI.

In the next chapter, we will look at a new breed of powerful AI models that are also inherently explainable. Because of this, we will look at neuro-symbolic AI and how it promises to address the issues mentioned so far.

5

Introducing Neuro-Symbolic AI
– the Next Level of AI

Throughout the previous chapters, we discussed how the primary motivation behind **artificial intelligence** (**AI**) is to model human intelligence into computer systems. Over the years, we have witnessed the innovation of many algorithms and techniques that improved computer cognitive and logical processing machines. In *Chapter 2*, we introduced symbolic AI as one of the first research efforts targeted toward achieving this highly desirable accolade. We discussed how symbolic AI has enabled us to embed world-knowledge constructs (logical rules) into our computer systems. However, the symbolic AI process has proven to be rather cumbersome and expensive. Researchers have also discovered that symbolic AI programs tend to lose accuracy as more rules are represented in the program. To circumvent the tedious process of symbolic rule representation, the field shifted its focus to more data-driven techniques.

Neural networks (**NNs**) and **deep learning** (**DL**) have solved multiple complex tasks, allowing us to push the boundaries of machine intelligence. Especially in computer vision and large-scale pattern recognition tasks, DL has shown itself to be wildly successful. Still, these algorithms struggle to extract and understand the compositional structure from the underlying data. Deep networks are unable to reason about the patterns that they learn. As such, explaining relationships between the different objects of a specific problem is a task that deep networks struggle to complete. While deep networks have closed the gap between machine and human intelligence, this limitation proves that we are still far from fully modeling human intelligence. One of the differentiating factors between man and machine is our ability to reason about common-sense knowledge—more specifically, our ability to understand concepts and their implications. The human brain can rapidly create complex associations. For example, seeing someone with headphones on, we automatically assume they probably cannot hear us if we speak to them.

This chapter aims to introduce the emerging concept of **neuro-symbolic AI** (**NSAI**), familiarize us with the different mechanics surrounding this innovation, and help us understand why NSAI is being seen by many as the way to go for future AI developments.

The first objective of this chapter is to understand the journey that led to the innovation behind NSAI. Next, we will learn the conceptual intuition behind NSAI. The main objective here is to understand the rationale behind NSAI research. Following this, we will discuss the different components encapsulated within the NSAI process. Learning the other ingredients and how they fit together is critical to correctly understanding how to design a robust NSAI architecture. Finally, we will briefly overview the principal techniques in the NSAI space.

This chapter will go through the following topics:

- Understanding the intuition behind NSAI

- Defining NSAI

- The components of an NSAI architecture

The idea behind NSAI

Bridging the intelligence gap between man and machine is our destination—the holy grail. The challenge of solving the physical brain's complexity has intrigued researchers for years. Over the years, we raised and answered numerous questions; nonetheless, one question still prevails. Scientists know that we cannot understand the brain's function to its entirety, especially its ability to develop common-sense knowledge—which essentially boils down to multiple complex associations that the brain can extract.

> **Defining common-sense knowledge**
>
> Common-sense knowledge is any knowledge that becomes almost second nature or apparent to us. For example, if we see a chair, we can practically assume we can sit on it. If we see a bed, we know that we can lie on it without falling through the mattress. The director of the MIT-IBM Watson AI Lab, David Cox, defines common-sense knowledge as *"all of the implicit knowledge that we have that is never written down anywhere."*

Solving the issue of having machines not just learn common sense but also fully *understand* it (and its underlying knowledge) seems to be the next step for the new generation of AI techniques. Machine-enabled knowledge understanding is the objective.

How can we ever model something that we do not fully understand?

Modeling human intelligence – insights from child psychology

Our target is to enable machines to reason like humans, to help machines deeply understand the characteristic of the objects within a particular problem set, to extract further information through reasoning, and to transition the field of AI from pattern recognition to cognition and reasoning. As humans, we can do much more than pattern recognition. We can imagine things, concepts, and designs. We can reason about things to plan actions and play out several scenarios that might never occur. The brain is our most complex organ. We still have a lot of mysteries to uncover about our neurology, so how can we imitate such complex functionality without us even understanding its implications?

Inspired by the aforementioned premise, researchers from the MIT-IBM collaboration decided that the best way to model this complexity was by approaching it the same way a human child develops brain function. Although we do not fully understand the human brain and its complex functionality, children still somehow develop their brains to reach such desired levels of intelligence. Throughout their brain development cycle, children manage to pick up on common-sense knowledge with very few examples. Gradually, they start forming relationships with the various objects in their surroundings and strengthen their abilities to reason about them. With a handful of instances, a baby can begin to recognize and differentiate between a cat and a dog—a task that would see an AI model requiring thousands of samples to reach accurate levels. As such, the starting point for this research becomes relatively straightforward—understanding the psychological development of human offspring. Researchers wanted to merge human psychology and neuroscience with AI.

Rebecca Saxe, a professor of cognitive neuroscience at MIT, sought to understand further how human babies viewed the world around them. How did they perceive it? How did they know it?

Babies are mainly considered relatively passive; initially, their abilities are limited. They cannot speak or walk. As with naïve **machine learning (ML)** or AI models, children start with slender intuition of the physical world. We then train these models by passively feeding them data points and allowing them to extract their patterns and structures. Quite like the human baby, no? Well, Saxe argues no. Babies are not born as passive entities. Babies are actively making decisions. Babies decide what they look at and what they focus their attention on. In turn, these decisions significantly impact the kinds of relationships and patterns babies can learn early on. **Near-Infrared Spectroscopy (NIRS)** is an experiment that studies neural activity through light. Light is shone through the subject's scalp, and detectors are used to measure the amount of reflected light. This test determines the brain's blood oxygenation levels, which indicate neuron activity. Using this experiment, researchers started monitoring and studying human baby cognition. Neural activity in a human baby was observed to be somewhat active. Especially when a human baby appears to be simply staring at an object, significant brain activity and development are occurring in the background. Babies might be staring at a particular thing because it might trigger different emotions (scared, surprised, or happy) or engage curiosity. A baby's gaze masks several mental activities. Our brain develops a model of our world composed of objects, agents, and interactions. The different agents are their entities, with their model of the world and their knowledge base.

Essentially, the next step was to research the confluence of AI and psychology to understand further how to model the human brain best. Through various studies conducted by psychology researchers Michael Tomasello and Felix Warneken, we know that children construct ideas about objects and agents in the physical world. They form knowledge of how the different agents interact with each other and things in the world. But most importantly, these studies show that children can improvise and adapt this knowledge to similar but novel scenarios. Children develop intuition. Joshua Tenenbaum argues that children start developing reasoning capabilities immediately after birth. Three months after birth, a human child would have developed common-sense intuition to bridge other intelligence parts, including language and planning skills.

> **The closet experiment**
>
> One of the experiments by Michael Tomasello and Felix Warneken involved a man carrying seemingly heavy books (with both hands) toward a closed closet. The man walked toward the closet and appeared to struggle to open the closet door. A child in the room picked up on the intended goal of the man and proceeded to help him by opening the closet door for him. Even though the child was not briefed on what to do, the child understood that the interaction between the man (an agent in the physical world) and the closet (an object in the physical world) was to open it and store the books inside. You can watch the experiment in action here: `https://videopress.com/v/xUifKHYO`.

Another point of inspiration was also drawn from observing mallard ducklings. Researchers noted how the ducklings understand the concept of similarity (or dissimilarity). If the ducklings are exposed to two similar objects (for example, two red balls) at birth, they will tend to follow or favor pairs of similar objects. Conversely, they will prefer dissimilar pairs if they are shown different things. In short, mallard ducklings are born with the intuitive ability to determine whether two foreign objects are similar. They can discover, learn, and abstract various properties and relationships that they can ultimately reason about. This task is something that, to this day, AI algorithms find rather difficult to learn.

Research also showed that, contrary to popular belief, humans are not born as blank canvases. Instead, we possess a pre-programmed basic understanding of the world. We are born with some innate knowledge of how the world operates. We are born with intuition about the approximation and simulation of our physical world. Researchers like to compare this concept with that of a game engine. The game engine encapsulates some knowledge of world physics and other fundamentals. It is then fine-tuned and enhanced to fit the desired world simulation. Human babies are thought to behave quite similarly. We are born with some innate knowledge of fundamental world relationships. Through life experiences (that is, newer data points), our internal "game engine" becomes more efficient in modeling real-life scenarios. As such, researchers believe that adopting specific probabilistic ideas from game engines can help advance this course.

The ingredients of an NSAI system

With AI gaining more traction, in August of 2019, strong research efforts began to enable common-sense and reasoning abilities in AI systems by reverse engineering the brain of human babies. As the name implies, the recipe of neuro-symbolic programming involves two main ingredients: NNs and symbolic programming. We will explore these two ingredients using the **Compositional Language and Elementary Visual Reasoning (CLEVR)** example case. CLEVR is a dataset of 100,000 computer-generated scenes portraying 3D shapes (`https://cs.stanford.edu/people/jcjohns/clevr/`). The objective of this dataset is for AI to reason about these images and be able to answer questions regarding the said images—for example: *How many spheres are in the image?*

The symbolic ingredient

Motivated by their observations, the researchers highlighted one key aspect of the reasoning abilities of humans (and other organisms, for that matter): world knowledge. We can reason about objects because we understand the underlying structure and relationships of the said objects. Albeit potentially not entirely, we possess some knowledge that allows us to question and reason about these objects. Researchers tend to be split over whether we have innate world knowledge or can simply learn this knowledge over time. Frankly speaking, as AI practitioners, it's superfluous. The main point of interest here is that to reason, we require knowledge—either direct or indirect. So, the first piece of the puzzle to enable machine reasoning is implementing a system to provide knowledge of the physical world to our AI model. This way, our AI can understand the dynamics and relationships of objects within its world model.

> **Note**
>
> The term *world* here refers to the problem space in which a specific AI is defined to solve a particular task.

If we recall our discussion from *Chapter 2*, one of the ideal candidates for this would be symbolic AI. symbolic AI allows us to provide our AI system with a structured (symbolic) representation of our problem space—the knowledge base. Nevertheless, we had already discussed how most symbolic AI approaches require tedious manual processes to define the knowledge base. We also discussed other limitations, such as the lack of scalability properties (that is, the constant need to update the knowledge base with new rules to reflect newly learned knowledge), as well as its dependency on manually defined formal rules. In our use case, as with the orange example in *Chapter 2*, building our knowledge base would require us to determine (through logical propositions) the various world properties. In general, we would need to manually define the various types of shapes in our world (that is, a sphere, a cylinder, or a cube), the different shape colors (that is, red, blue, or yellow), shape sizes (that is, large or small), and their texture (that is, metallic or gloss). We also need to formalize the different relationships. For instance, if two objects have the same shape, they are similar. We can immediately start to appreciate the level of complexity and abstraction required to represent our domain fully. *Figure 5.1* illustrates an example symbolic AI framework for this use case:

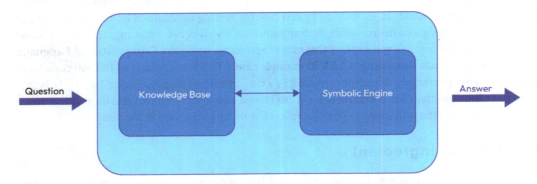

Figure 5.1: An example symbolic AI framework

One significant issue becomes apparent in this example. If we were to show the AI a scene with a new shape (or any other of the defined properties), our symbolic AI program would fail. For symbolic AI to be efficient, these limitations must be addressed. As a result, given its ability to enable human-like reasoning and strong explainability properties, researchers sought to improve on these limitations. So, they asked themselves this question:

Can we exploit symbolic AI and improve its limitations to enable human-like reasoning in machines?

The primary angle to make symbolic AI drastically better would be to take the human effort out of the equation; thus, we would need to figure out how to design, structure, and build the knowledge base automatically. This point brings us to our second component: NNs.

The neural ingredient

As discussed in *Chapter 3*, one of the biggest strengths of NNs is their ability to learn complex patterns and relationships from raw datasets. These intricate patterns should, in theory, provide enough information within their neural connections to describe the world we are trying to model. In our example, we would train any NN architecture to learn complex patterns within our input. In this case, the input would be 3D shape images, with the output being the objects within the image. We show a simple architecture of this network in *Figure 5.2*:

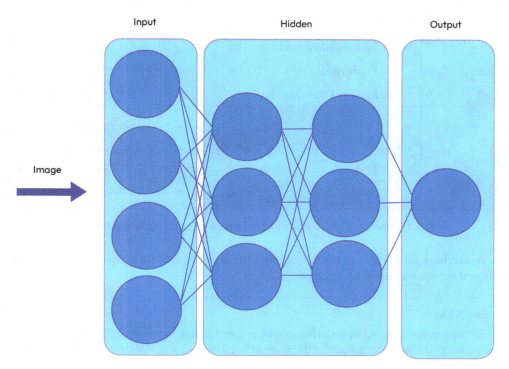

Figure 5.2: An example of a NN connection

The main limitation of NNs is the lack of reasoning abilities. With the preceding network, having the network reason and answer questions on objects within the image is rather challenging. Although the NN can learn the patterns and characteristics of various things, it does not understand anything beyond that. We can train a NN model with enough training data to answer questions and enable reasoning. However, this process would require a substantial amount of both computing resources and training data.

With these limitations in mind, the question we want to answer becomes the following:

Can we exploit the pattern recognition powers of NNs to extract symbolic patterns from our data automatically?

Once we affirm this question, we can have these NNs automatically build our knowledge base.

The neuro-symbolic blend

If we take a holistic overview of the current situation, we immediately realize that the strengths of symbolic AI directly target the weaknesses imposed by NNs and vice versa. We detail a summarized overview of these strengths and weaknesses in *Table 5.1*, as follows:

	Strength	Weakness
Symbolic AI	<ul><li>Human-like reasoning</li><li>Explainable</li><li>Smaller knowledge base</li></ul>	<ul><li>A manual and tedious process</li><li>Difficult to scale</li></ul>
NN	<ul><li>Automated pattern extraction</li><li>Scalable</li></ul>	<ul><li>Unable to reason</li><li>Abstract and complex to interpret</li><li>Large dataset</li></ul>

Table 5.1: Summary of strengths and weaknesses of Symbolic AI and NNs

As such, researchers got the idea to combine these two parent AI techniques to create a hybrid AI architecture that improves upon both methods.

> **Defining NSAI**
>
> NSAI (or neuro-symbolic AI or neural-symbolic or subsymbolic-symbolic AI) is a composite AI framework that seeks to merge the domains of Symbolic AI and NNs to create a superior hybrid AI model possessing reasoning capabilities.

Mainly pushed by the MIT-IBM collaboration, the NSAI architecture seeks to combine the features of both its parent techniques, as outlined here:

- In Symbolic AI, we must implement the knowledge base, and then the AI (driven by an inference engine sitting on top of the knowledge base) can be used to answer questions
- In NNs, we train the model to arrive at the correct answer autonomously

As such, the hybrid NSAI architecture is designed so that a NN is used to automatically build the part of the knowledge base required to answer user questions. So, what does the NSAI paradigm look like when applied to our 3D shapes example? Let's have a look:

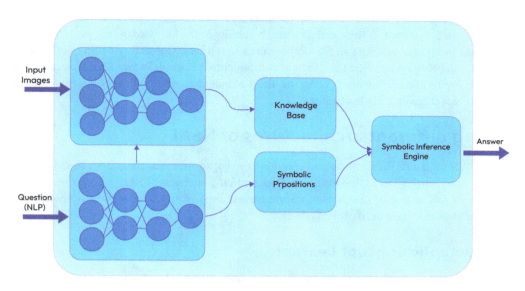

Figure 5.3: A schematic example of the hybrid NSAI architecture

In the preceding diagram, we show the components within the NSAI architecture that combine the NN domain with that of Symbolic AI. We further summarize the steps involved in this architecture, as follows:

1. Train a NN on the images to learn and understand the various properties and relationships that define the shapes within the images.

2. This network is used to generate the knowledge base.

3. In our example, user questions are submitted as plain English text. We need another **natural language processing** (**NLP**) process to transform these questions into symbolic propositions.

4. The symbolic propositions are fed into the **symbolic inference engine** (**SIE**).

5. The SIE provides an answer.

We can look at the NSAI concept using a similar mindset to the initial Symbolic AI approach. The main target objective remains to provide machines with knowledge of the world. We still want to enable machine intelligence through machine reasoning by allowing the machine to map symbolic relations.

When designing an NSAI system, the thought process should still focus on how best to enable the machine to understand its problem space thoroughly. However, our approach to generating the world's symbolic knowledge differs. In retrospect, the Symbolic AI paradigm remains quite strong. Maybe its failure resulted from Symbolic AI being too ahead of its time. In the same way that DL was significantly limited and held back by computing hardware technology, maybe Symbolic AI was being held back by a lack of software focus. As such, the perspective when building an NSAI framework versus a Symbolic AI system should not vary drastically.

In an NSAI architecture, we still need the SEI to handle user requests and yield results. NNs are simply leveraged to allow greater scalability, flexibility, and reliability in the knowledge base underlying the SEI. This is not to say that building an NSAI system is a trivial task. Correctly defining the suitable architectures and bridging between the different components is critical. In any AI architecture, we heavily rely on inputs of one component being the direct output of another. Still, in NSAI, this concept is even more evident, given its hybrid nature.

Exploring different architectures of NSAI

Although NSAI is still a relatively niche and emerging field of study, researchers from the MIT-IBM collaboration and Google's DeepMind have already contributed interesting research concerning NSAI architectures. In this section of the chapter, we will further explore and discuss some of these main NSAI architectures that have been proven effective.

Neuro-Symbolic Concept Learner

The main objective of the **Neuro-Symbolic Concept Learner** (**NSCL**) architecture is to produce a model capable of learning to identify objects in an image and parsing and understanding their semantics and linking relationships [3]. NSCL is based on the concept that humans can understand visual concepts through their ability to bridge between vision and language. For example, let us assume we are shown a photo of a blue elephant. We immediately identify that the "object" captured in the picture is an elephant. We also understand that the color of the said elephant is blue. Somehow, we can symbolize visual objects into their constituting properties, such as color. Recall that this process is essentially the human brain taking in a visual concept and splitting it into several symbolic propositions. That is how we can think of the word *blue* when we see blue. Furthermore, our mind can join the relationships between our vision and senses with language and semantics. The result of this ability is a mind that is spatially and referentially aware—a mind that can comprehend the physical world.

NSCL seeks to replicate this complex processing through a concept that the authors call *object-based scene representation*. In simple terms, this concept means that given a particular image, NSCL can identify and segregate the objects within that image and reason about them. NSCL can achieve this remarkable feat through a three-step hybrid model composed of an *image parser*, a *question parser*, and a *symbolic executor*. The NSAI architecture we previously discussed (refer to *Figure 5.3*) is based on the NSCL model. The NSCL model was trained using the aforementioned CLEVR dataset (that is, a set of images, questions, and their respective answers). Let us dive deeper into the sub-models of NSCL.

The image parser sub-model

The image parser sub-model is a form of NN designed to learn from the images and the provided question-answer pairs provided. The NN defined in this research was based on a mask **region-based convolutional NN** (**R-CNN**) using the ResNet-34 model architecture for object recognition and segmentation (that is, masking). This model also enables spatially aware learning and other contextual relative properties such as object size. Newer implementations also use Meta's Detectron2 model

(Meta's computer vision platform provides several object detection and segmentation models—refer to https://ai.facebook.com/tools/detectron2/).

There are no labels involved throughout the training process. Instead, the NN learns to infer object representations and other visual concepts (such as the color and shape) of the said objects to create the image annotations themselves. Next, the NN starts learning more straightforward concepts, such as differentiating between two colors or contrasting shapes. Also, the network begins with relatively simple scenes, showing a small number of shapes (or even a single shape). From there, the NN adopts an incremental learning strategy whereby the complexity of the visual concepts is increased. For instance, the NN might now focus on understanding more complex attributes based on spatial and relational awareness cues (for example, object X is on top of object Y).

Finally, the network could join and understand more complex questions involving multiple visual cues. For example, given a scene with numerous shapes of varying colors, the model is asked to give the color of the large cylinder to the right of the blue sphere. This training process mimics how we typically teach the human brain—especially babies. We adopt a curriculum that sequentially increases in difficulty and complexity, and where the next topic or concept continues to build on top of the previous one.

The question parser sub-model

One of the main challenges surrounding the CLEVR dataset is understanding natural language questions to provide an accurate answer. For the NSAI model to reason and answer queries, it must first understand the object and scene properties (achieved by the first sub-model) and the question. In the NSCL architecture, the latter was accomplished using a custom **Domain-Specific Language (DSL)**.

What is a DSL?

A DSL can be thought of as a computer language that serves the purpose of a specific domain. Unlike a language such as English (which is a general-purpose language), a DSL only makes sense (and can be understood) by experts in a particular field. Some DSL examples include the web's **HyperText Markup Language (HTML)** and **Structured Query Language (SQL)** for database management systems.

The researchers of NSCL built their DSL for understanding questions, reasoning about visual concepts, and coming up with an answer. The DSL allowed definitions for properties such as FILTER (filters out objects based on the parameter—that is, FILTER(BLUE) will filter out all blue shapes) or QUERY (allows us to query a specific attribute of a particular object—that is, QUERY(OBJ1, SHAPE)). A full list of the operations defined by this DSL can be found at http://nscl.csail.mit.edu/data/papers/2019ICLR-NSCL.pdf. The model selected for this NLP task was a bidirectional **Gated Recurrent Unit (GRU)**. The GRU is responsible for the semantic parsing of the original natural language question into the DSL executable statement.

The symbolic executor sub-model

The final sub-model to this hybrid process is the symbolic executor. For this last part, we require the parsed executable program from the DSL semantic parsing step and a trained image parser for object masking. The objective of this module is to take these artifacts as input and generate the corresponding answer based on learned object visual concepts. In the NSCL architecture, the symbolic executor is said to be quasi-symbolic. Unlike a fully symbolic AI system, the NSCL symbolic executor does not perform Boolean operations on the knowledge base. Instead, this symbolic executor relies on probabilistic computation to generate differentiable results. In short, every object in the scene is given a probability value representing the likelihood that that object is selected to be part of the final output. For the sake of comprehension, we illustrate this entire process (in a simplified manner) in *Figure 5.4*, as follows.

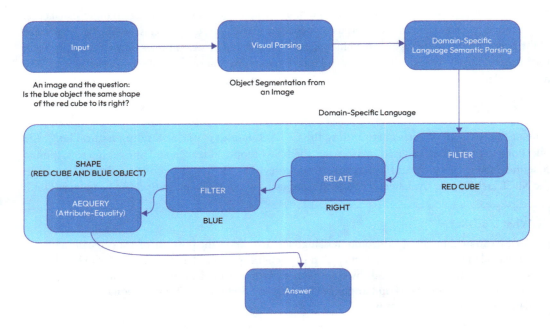

Figure 5.4: An overview of the NSCL architecture (source: adapted from Mao et al.)

Neuro-symbolic dynamic reasoning

The CLEVR dataset proved essential in setting a standard for NSAI research, providing a valid reason for going after NSAI research and a virtual platform to evaluate the solutions globally. After the development of NSCL, researchers took the concept of NSCL and CLEVR a step further. The **CoLlision Events for Video REpresentation and Reasoning (CLEVRER)** dataset (`http://clevrer.csail.mit.edu`) was introduced to build upon the CLEVR dataset by moving from images to videos [4]. As with CLEVR, CLEVRER is based on computer-generated 3D shapes. The dataset includes several 5-second videos showing objects moving around, colliding with each other, entering the frame, and exiting the frame. This dataset introduces an interesting variable in the equation of complex reasoning—**causality**. Given a video, we are now exposing the NSAI model to a whole new spectrum of relationships based on cause and effect. For example, objects can collide with each other, so we might want to ask the model to tell us which objects have collided. The authors even targeted a more complex composition, asking the network if a different scenario or event had occurred, would the same objects still have collided?

The dynamics predictor sub-model

The existing network architectures could not reason about these more complex queries because of a lack of physics knowledge. Therefore, the **Neuro-Symbolic Dynamic Reasoning (NSDR)** architecture is the NSCL model with an extra sub-model as a physics engine. Researchers refer to this new sub-model as the **Dynamics Predictor (DP)** since its central role is to learn and understand object force propagation (that is, how force is produced and transferred between objects).

Based on a **Propagation Network (PropNet)** model (a learnable physics simulation engine based on DL—refer to `http://propnet.csail.mit.edu`), the DP module can model and predict the trajectory and positional reference of different objects and, therefore, can mathematically compute expected collisions from crossing trajectories. Another benefit enabled by PropNet is that it can approximate object motion even with missing information. This property is crucial to the CLEVRER dataset since an object can move in and out of frame. Thus, we could still approximate the object's trajectory, understand its cause and effect on the other trajectories, and reason about it. This module of the model also serves the purpose of explainability, besides enabling deep reasoning capabilities ranging from descriptive (such as NSCL—colors and object counts) to predicting the next event. In addition to counterfactual reasoning (how would the outcome change if a new event were to happen), the model can also explain why an external event would have prevented a collision (for example, the external event would have disrupted the trajectory of an object that would have crossed paths with another object).

The remaining sub-models

The DP sub-model is, perhaps, the main attraction to the NSDR architecture. However, this is not to say that the other sub-models were left unchanged from the NSCL model. Instead, we will discuss the changes to the remaining sub-models to make the newer NSAI architecture play nice with CLEVRER.

The video parser

The hybrid approach's first step is learning to make sense of the inputs. In the NSCL architecture, we had an image parser module that served the purpose of object masking. In NSDR, our inputs have now changed from a single image to a collection of images (frames) to form a video. NSDR considers every single frame of every video individually. In turn, NSDR still uses the same mask R-CNN network implemented for the NSCL model to perform object masking on every frame. Every clip in the CLEVRER dataset is composed of 25 frames. Hence, for every clip, the mask R-CNN must be executed 25 times.

The question parser

The questions in CLEVRER contain longer (and more complex) sequences than those of CLEVR. As such, the original **sequence-to-sequence (Seq2Seq)** model used by NSCL was replaced with a more modern architecture based on the **Long Short-Term Memory (LSTM)** encoder. Nevertheless, the question parser of NSDR works quite similarly to the NSCL one. We use the LSTM network to translate an English query into a functional program based on custom DSL.

> **Understanding the Seq2Seq model**
>
> As the name implies, a Seq2Seq model takes in a sequence as its input and outputs another sequence. The sequence can be anything from text, characters, pixel information, and time series. Examples of Seq2Seq models include translation models (given a phrase in one language, the model will output its translated version to another language), image captioning (a sequence of pixel information as input and a sequence of text as output), and text summarization (a sequence of text as input and another sequence of text as output).

The symbolic executor

Perhaps the second most prominent change in the NSDR architecture compared to that of NSCL lies within this module. If you recall, the **symbolic executor (SE)** program of NSCL was quasi-symbolic since it was based on probabilistic computations. This change shifts the learning focus from the SE program onto the video parser and the DP modules. Given its fully symbolic nature, the role of the SE program is purely to generate the respective answer based on the outputs of the previous modules. The answer is formed through an iteration of functional programming steps (filtering and logical operations). You can see the following diagram [4]:

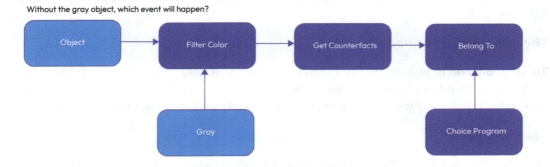

Figure 5.5: An example SE program of NSDR

In recent years, another NSAI architecture—the **Neural Logic Machine (NLM)**—has started to gain some popularity within the research community. The NLM is an NSAI architecture (as shown in *Figure 5.6*), presented and unofficially maintained by Google (https://sites.google.com/view/neural-logic-machines). We discuss this architecture further in the following section.

Dissecting the NLM architecture

The NLM architecture is a fully differentiable approach capable of first-order logic. The NLM process starts with logical predicates describing a fixed collection of objects. The first task of the NLM is to extract the various object properties and relations from the given logical propositions. The result of this can be thought of as our knowledge base since they define the properties of our world objects and their mutual relations. These predicates can be of three main types, as follows:

- **Binary**—Defines some object relationships. For example, `BELOW(X, Y)` means that object X is below object Y.

- **Nullary**—Defines global properties. For example, `ALLMATCHED()` means that all objects match each other.

- **Unary**—Defines individual object properties. For example, `TRANSPARENT(X)` means that object X is transparent.

The neurons in a NN perform all their computation through tensors. A tensor is a data structure that encodes multidimensional arrays and performs mathematical operations on them. A tensor can be used to represent data with complex relationships such as images and text. Therefore, the NLM architecture represents these logical propositions as probabilistic tensors whose respective logical rules and connectives are transformed into neural operators. Through a forward propagation approach (consisting of several highly abstracted **Multi-Layer Perceptrons** (**MLPs**) performing several expansion and reduction operations), the NLM can achieve first-order logic deduction, discovering more profound object properties and relationships. In short, the NLM process starts with a set of predicate logic statements, performs logic deduction, and generates conclusive object concepts. NLM has succeeded in a few applications, including pathfinding (finding the most optimal route between two points), array sorting (arranging the elements in an array in a specific order), and the block world problem [1]. You can see an overview of the NLM architecture in the following diagram:

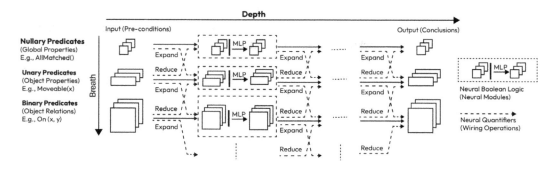

Figure 5.6: An overview of the NLM architecture (adapted from Dong et al.[2])

Summary

NSAI is the new kid on the block in the field of AI. NSAI is considered by many as the next level of AI, or the new AI revolution, mainly due to its ability to equip machines with human-like reasoning capabilities.

This chapter started by venturing through human psychology's vast and exciting realm. We briefly explored the human reasoning process and discussed how humans and other beings develop the ability to understand and reason about physical world objects early on. Common-sense knowledge seems to be an innate skill that humans possess—or at least one that we can learn autonomously to a certain degree. We then dissected the hybrid NSAI model into its constituent parents: Symbolic AI and NNs. NNs seem to have granted Symbolic AI a second chance to prove itself as a worthy contender for achieving the original motivation behind AI systems—reaching human levels of reasoning intelligence in computers. Further, we also discussed the NSCL, NSDR, and NLM architectures, the main current frameworks behind NSAI research efforts.

In the following chapter, we will discuss further the obstacles and opportunities of NSAI, some of its implications, and the future direction of NSAI research.

Further reading

Following are a few resources for you to dive deeper into the concepts discussed in the chapter:

1. *Principles of artificial intelligence*, Nilsson, Nils J., 1933.

2. *Neural Logic Machines* in International Conference on Learning Representations, by Honghua Dong, Jiayuan Mao, Tian Lin, Chong Wang, Lihong Li, and Denny Zhou (2019).

3. *The Neuro-Symbolic Concept Learner: Interpreting Scenes, Words, and Sentences From Natural Supervision*, ICLR 2019, by Mao, J., Gan, C., Kohli, P., Tenenbaum, J.B., and Wu, J..

4. *CLEVRER: CoLlision Events for Video REpresentation and Reasoning* by Yi, K., Gan, C., Li, Y., Kohli, P., Wu, J., Torralba, A., and Tenenbaum, J.B..

5. *Neuro-Symbolic AI: An Emerging Class of AI Workloads and their Characterization* by Susskind, Z., Arden, B., John, L.K., Stockton, P., and John, E.B..

6

A Marriage of Neurons and Symbols – Opportunities and Obstacles

Research interest in **neuro-symbolic artificial intelligence (NSAI)** is on the rise. Currently, most researchers and **artificial intelligence (AI)** practitioners rely on **deep learning (DL)** algorithms as solutions to their tasks. The drawbacks and limitations have been widely documented, ranging from extremely resource-hungry processes to ambiguous and complex inner mechanics rendering a certain lack of interpretability. The modern generation acknowledges the importance of producing systems that we can fully understand. We also understand the significance of developing efficient processes that can achieve high-performance levels with fewer resources. For example, the craze of cryptocurrency (especially Bitcoin) mining saw a huge spike in computing electricity consumption worldwide. Forbes estimates that Bitcoin mining consumes roughly 127 terawatt-hours of electricity annually. To put this into perspective, that is greater than the total annual power consumption of some countries such as Norway, the Netherlands, and the United Arab Emirates! (Refer to https://www.forbes.com/advisor/investing/cryptocurrency/bitcoins-energy-usage-explained/). Especially with the current political turmoil and the electricity crisis that the world is experiencing, the need for designing and developing sustainable, efficient, and scalable systems is proving to be detrimental.

The area of NSAI is quite promising, and some researchers are positioning NSAI to be the next revolution in the sphere of AI. As we previously discussed, the domain of AI (like most other fields of study) tends to go through various highs and lows of innovative progress (winters and summers). Most researchers believe that we are currently in an AI spring. The field of AI is well funded with strong interest. However, innovation feels like it's slowing down.

DL has been around for some time now, and although we have witnessed some remarkable state-of-the-art breakthroughs thanks to DL, it still feels like we are missing something. This feeling is perhaps why the rise of NSAI has piqued the attention of several researchers. NSAI is hoping to help take us from the spring season to summer.

One of the ultimate objectives of AI is reaching the level of general AI – meaning that we no longer build specialized AI systems that can perform a single task but rather build an entity capable of performing several general tasks. Think of it like a humanoid robot that possesses all basic human skills. Researchers believe that NSAI can take us there thanks to its number of improvements over the DL family of techniques.

No technique or solution is perfect. Trade-offs will always exist, and compromises will always need to be taken. The goal of this chapter is to investigate the trade-offs involved when combining symbolic reasoning and DL. It will highlight why NSAI is providing hope to solve even more complex problems. Throughout this chapter, we will also discuss the main limitations currently faced by neuro-symbolic computing.

The first objective of this chapter is to deeply understand the motivation behind NSAI in terms of what it has to offer. We will discuss the current limitations of NSAI and the future research direction.

This chapter will go through the following topics:

- The opportunities presented to us by NSAI

- The current limitations and obstacles of NSAI

- The current research gaps in NSAI

The benefits of combining neurons and symbols

In the previous chapter, we mentioned several key elements that make NSAI attractive to researchers. The idea of merging two parent AI techniques and trimming away all their limitations sounds rather promising. NSAI research has explored this new generation of AI workers under different lights – each highlighting various opportunities presented by NSAI. Having said that, as argued by the director of the MIT-IBM Watson AI research lab, Dr. Cox, we can group the benefits of NSAI into three main categories. Throughout this section, we will introduce each of these categories and delve further into how they are accomplished by NSAI.

Data efficiency

There is no denying that **neural networks** (**NNs**) have been the key to multiple state-of-the-art solutions. There is no denying the powerful capabilities offered by NNs to solve highly complex problems. However, NNs are incredibly data-hungry. As we discussed in the previous chapters, NNs require huge amounts of data to achieve the incredible performance figures that we so desire. This data-hungry characteristic of NNs renders them unusable in multiple use cases.

Out in the real world, especially in the business world, we are often faced with two main scenarios: no data and expensive data. Let's consider some use cases.

Scenario A – no data

The use case is a data scientist at a **business-to-business** (**B2B**) start-up company developing a **customer relationship management** (**CRM**) platform for other businesses. The company manages a data warehouse that monitors customers' general information and their respective transaction history. The data warehouse is populated through several data ingestion processes. The CEO of the company approaches you and asks you to build a fraud detection system to flag fraudulent transactions as part of the CRM platform. There are no collected samples of known fraudulent cases and the business does not currently have a team of fraud analysts set up. What do you do?

The short answer here is probably not much. Yes, more experienced data scientists can be creative and explore the problem from other angles. You might try unsupervised approaches to separate the customers based on their past transactions, or maybe even consult third-party datasets to help build a dataset for modeling. Lately, **Generative Adversarial Networks** (**GANs**) have also grown in popularity for generating synthetic datasets to use for model training. However, irrespective of the approach you end up taking, the outcome is highly likely to be inferior to a model that had access to the right data. In this case, the business per se does not currently have access to the right data; they may need to consult with other supplemental data sources. Solving the lack of data in this scenario can be done, but it is a time-consuming process with questionable performance.

Scenario highlights:

- Access to no data points
- Possible to collect new data points, but the process is time-consuming (and potentially manually exhaustive)

Scenario B – expensive data

The use case is that you are a data scientist working in the health industry. A novel virus has been declared a pandemic in the past few days and everyone is in panic mode, causing health responders to become overwhelmed. The CEO asks you to work on a system that, given a set of symptoms and other patient details, determines whether the patient requires hospitalization or not. Only a handful of research studies have been published investigating the various symptoms caused by the virus and their respective severity.

Here, we have no past data to exploit since this is a novel virus. However, we can leverage the mentioned research to build a small dataset. We can probably also attempt to draw influence from past similar events. Collecting new data points is incredibly time-consuming (almost impossible unless we have access to direct sources) and costly.

Scenario highlights:

- Access to no or few data points
- Collecting new data points is difficult, incredibly time-consuming, and expensive

Small data is the new cool

In the past few years, we have witnessed the introduction of a new buzzword: **big data**. Everyone wanted it. No one knew what it meant. The data age was quickly transforming how businesses operate and leverage data. The focus was on adopting systems that can handle huge volumes of data and coming in at (seemingly) high velocity. Nowadays, businesses are starting to realize that a significant portion of their problems falls within the confines of scenarios A and B, which we discussed previously.

Building complex NNs using millions of data points suddenly lost its wow factor, mainly because most business problems don't have millions of rows of data points to begin with. Even more so today, both businesses and researchers are attracted to the idea of achieving high levels of performance using smaller datasets. Perhaps this is one of the most intriguing benefits of NSAI techniques. If you recall *Chapter 5*, we discussed how one of the standard datasets used for NSAI was the CLEVR dataset. The researchers there evaluated their NSAI architectures against other state-of-the-art NN techniques. The NSAI framework reached high accuracy levels (significantly outperforming the other algorithms) with training on just 1% of the entire dataset. Using 10% of the dataset, NSAI achieved an almost perfect score of 99.8%!

Combining symbolic knowledge with neurons ultimately creates a beautiful harmony in training. The symbolic paradigm allows the NN to generalize faster and better when training on smaller datasets by regularizing it. Through NSAI, this smaller data is essentially reduced to a point where every single observation within that dataset represents its entity – its group. This behavior is mainly achieved through the symbolic program that is used to decompose the dataset into its constituent objects and relationships. The NSAI framework no longer requires seeing several instances of the same object or entity to learn its underlying structure. Rather, the symbolic execution enables it efficient enough to map its properties almost immediately with every sample it sees. Think about it – NSAI attempts to mimic human reasoning and thought processes. As humans, we do not need huge amounts of examples to learn a concept and understand its dynamics. As an analogy, consider *Figure 6.1*, which depicts a completely fictional and made-up object. Let's creatively call this new object *Four-Shapes*.

Figure 6.1: The Four-Shapes object, a fictional shape

Although this is the first time we're seeing this object, we can still answer questions and reason quite effortlessly about it. Consider the two depictions as part of *Figure 6.2*:

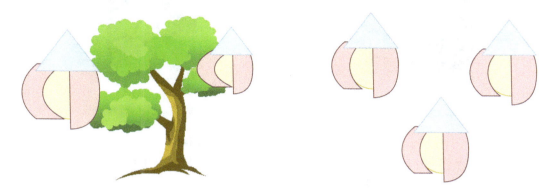

Figure 6.2: Left – two Four-Shapes of varying sizes and a tree; right – three identical Four-Shapes

If someone were to ask you to count the number of Four-Shapes on the right-hand side, you would easily answer three (hopefully!). If the same question was asked about the left-hand side, we would also be able to answer correctly (that is, two). Even though the left image depicts the shapes in addition to another object (in this case, a tree), and varying sizes, our brain can still process, associate, and recognize the individual objects. If you look closely at the left image, you will realize that the smaller Four-Shape is slightly different than the others in the sense that left part of the shape is slightly more curved. However, we still would count this as a *Four-Shape* object.

When we see the first sample of the new object (as shown in *Figure 6.1*), our brain immediately begins to decompose the shape into its different properties. Although we do not understand how it relates to the physical world (for example, does it grow on trees?), we can still quickly identify it in other scenarios. We can still reason about it and visualize it in different positions and orientations. Our brain has already built the "symbolic program" representing that object. We don't need to see hundreds or thousands of images to start recognizing it. This property is one that NSAI is trying to replicate.

High accuracy

At this point, it is pretty much overstated that NNs have resulted in state-of-the-art solutions over the years. While that is true, some of the results obtained by DL are also arguably overstated. Consider the computer vision domain. It is perhaps the area that benefited the most from DL innovation. It is also believed by many that modern DL solutions have almost perfected computer vision – even capable of beating humans!

Now, consider the following scenarios:

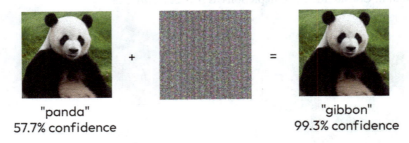

"panda"
57.7% confidence

"gibbon"
99.3% confidence

Figure 6.3: The panda versus gibbon adversarial attack
(adapted from Goodfellow, I.J., Shlens, J., and Szegedy, C. (2015) Explaining
and Harnessing Adversarial Examples, CoRR, abs/1412.6572)

The first example is shown in *Figure 6.3*. We start with an image of a panda. When passed to the state-of-the-art NN, we get a correct classification back with 57.7% confidence. If we were to add some imperceptible noise to the image, as depicted in the preceding figure, we would end up with an image that, to the human eye, remains identical to the original. We can all agree that the resultant image still shows a panda. However, the same NN is now 99.3% confident that this new image shows a gibbon.

The second example comes from the MIT-IBM curated ObjectNet dataset. The dataset was built using Amazon's Mechanical Turk (MTurk) – a freelancing platform. The MIT-IBM researchers paid MTurk freelancers to take photos of various objects with two main characteristics: the objects should not be the center of attention (for example, they should be positioned in the photo's corner), and their background should be different from the typical one (for example, a kitchen knife on a bathroom sink). State-of-the-art networks (which enjoyed a 97% accuracy on the ImageNet database) only achieved around 55% accuracy. Humans achieved over 90% on the same dataset. There are plenty of other documented examples where researchers succeeded in fooling an NN, including changing the color of a stop sign from red to brown causing it to not be detected by the NN (refer to `https://link.springer.com/chapter/10.1007/978-3-030-10925-7_4`) and fooling a human recognition system into using a custom t-shirt (refer to `https://link.springer.com/chapter/10.1007/978-3-030-58558-7_39`).

For this reason, DL is thought of as an 80-20 solution; it can get it right in 80% of the cases. The remaining 20% is often a combination of prediction error and black swan samples.

> **What is a black swan event?**
>
> This is a super rare scenario within the problem space that tends to have significant repercussions. Black swan events are deemed by many as impossible to predict due to their extreme rarity; however, their impact can be catastrophic.

The director of the MIT-IBM Watson AI research lab, Dr. Cox, discussed the burning traffic light scenario as a great example of a black swan event. Consider a self-driving car approaching a busy intersection. The traffic lights at this junction are on fire. The probability that the self-driving car had a burning traffic light in its training sample is slim to none. As such, the probability that the self-driving car ignores the traffic light could potentially be rather high. One outcome of this negligence would see the self-driving car continuing through the intersection without stopping and being involved in a crash. Even though most of us have never really seen a burning traffic light (and probably won't), if we ever were to encounter one, we would intuitively know how to act. We would know to stop and look out for oncoming traffic. We would wait for a safe moment to cross the intersection and proceed with extreme caution. As mentioned regarding the data efficiency argument, the human brain can quickly add one and two together to improvise a solution – even if we've never been in that specific situation before.

This task is something that NNs haven't managed to get right. So far, researchers have observed how the symbolic component of an NSAI framework aids this process. Through symbolical integration, the machine would learn the inner embeddings of the world, resulting in two main achievements:

- Improved object reasoning capabilities
- Improved generalization and performance (especially on smaller datasets, as mentioned previously)

As with most things NSAI, the dynamics of integrating symbolic reasoning with an NN is still being studied. Nonetheless, the current research shows that NSAI does provide a degree of reasoning capabilities. The symbolic representation of objects and relationships renders the AI capable of information extrapolation beyond any previously observed knowledge. In *Chapter 5*, we discussed the CLEVRER study (refer to the *Neuro-symbolic dynamic reasoning* section). Here, the NSAI framework exhibited the ability to reason about the objects' trajectories to answer counterfactual questions.

Transparency and interpretability

In *Chapter 4*, we discussed the field of **Explainable AI** (**XAI**) and its importance. We are living in a world dominated by technology – technology that is mostly powered by AI techniques. Most of us can agree that we need to seriously start regulating the field and holding machine learning accountable. It's no longer enough to say, "Because the AI said so." Any business and societal decision carries diverse critical and ethical considerations and the decision-maker must be fully aware of the entire thought process of any underlying algorithm.

Interpretability allows auditability. Auditability ensures fairness.

A byproduct of combining symbolic reasoning and an NN is a highly performant architecture thanks to the NN component, and a highly transparent system enabled by the symbolic component. It's widely known that a trade-off typically exists in machine learning: the higher the complexity of the algorithm, the lower its transparency. A linear regression model offers strong interpretability properties but lacks predictive power. On the other end of the spectrum, an NN offers strong predictive power but significantly lacks interpretation.

NSAI is promising in the sense that it offers the best of both worlds. The symbolic knowledge fed to the NN can ultimately provide the required transparency to understand its outcome. Let's consider a CLEVRER use case again. Consider a scene with three balls: one red, one blue, and one yellow. The scene depicts the red ball colliding with the blue ball. We ask the NSAI the counterfactual question, *"What if the yellow ball hits the red ball from the side before it collides with the blue ball?"*

The NSAI architecture possesses a certain degree of intuitive knowledge of our physical world. As we discussed, the NSAI can reason about the various physical and spatial properties encapsulated without that specific scenario. The NSAI starts to map out the initially expected trajectory paths of the different balls. Plugging the counterfactual knowledge in which the yellow ball will hit the red ball, the NSAI system will start to adjust the objects' projected movement and infer new paths. Through the symbolic component, the NSAI system knows that if an object is hit from its side, a change in momentum and direction is expected. All these considerations are represented within the network as symbolic propositions that we can access. Through symbolic representation, we can trace the network's reasoning step by step – rendering it highly transparent and interpretable.

It is believed that for a system to be interpretable, it also needs to be constrained. More specifically, it needs to be limited using domain-specific constraints – rules that correctly define and represent the domain so that a domain expert can easily understand it. The symbolic component of NSAI does just that!

The benefits promised by the NSAI paradigm are nothing short of remarkable. It promises the best of both worlds (symbolic reasoning and deep learning). NSAI holds the potential to revolutionize how we think about implementing AI systems. However, the NSAI framework still faces several challenges and limitations that cannot be ignored. In the next section, we will study the main obstacles that we must address to fully leverage the power of NSAI workers.

The challenges of combining neurons and symbols

So far, we have discussed the inner dynamics of NSAI and how this new class of computing promises to take machine intelligence to the next level. There are, however, a few obstacles that we need to overcome when designing an NSAI system. In this section, we will delve into the most prominent challenges and limitations of NSAI.

Knowledge and symbolic representation

Perhaps one of the more prominent obstacles to face when designing NSAI systems is knowledge and symbol representation. As part of the symbolic component, we have two main challenges:

- Robustly decomposing our problem space into symbols
- Representing the extracted symbols in a way that a computer (more specifically, an NN) can understand

In the previous chapters, we discussed how existing NSAI algorithms mostly rely on a **domain-specific language (DSL)** to represent the symbols and their respective relations as first-order logic. The DSL acts as a descriptor language of sorts to get this done through propositional logic – like the domain of inductive logic programming. Finding the optimal way to express both the symbolic relationships and their logical representations is perhaps the most challenging task of NSAI since this influences the rest of the architecture. The DSL should fulfill the following criteria:

- The specific description language must be rich enough to appropriately cater to varying levels of abstraction of the logical propositions

- It must be compositionally discrete (that is, capable of extrapolating logical knowledge beyond the existing or available data distribution) and fully explain the underlying local NN

- Its rules must be correct and logically sound, and must efficiently represent the underlying relationships

- For the sake of scalability and efficiency, the description language that's selected must be as simple as possible

This open challenge is significantly limited by the constantly increasing complexity of tasks to solve. As a result, the main challenge here is to define a description language capable of handling the growing logical complexity while keeping the integrity and expressivity of the extracted logical propositions.

Multi-source knowledge reasoning

The majority of the current NSAI efforts are focused on knowledge extraction from some source of data. Suppose we are trying to solve a particular problem for which we have multiple sources of data. Let's say that we have a set of unstructured text documents and structured tabular data. How can we combine and leverage both data sources for knowledge extraction and, in turn, build our symbolic knowledge base? This question is particularly difficult to answer.

The challenge here is to design a description language capable of extracting symbolic representations from both sources. Both data sources would likely have different data structures, encapsulate different relationships, and exhibit different data properties. Although both sources might represent knowledge on the same target objective, the characteristics of that knowledge might be different. The simple solution would be to design two different NSAI architectures (one for every source of data).

However, this strategy won't get us far. Firstly, it suffers from significant scalability issues. What if we had 10 different data sources? Or maybe 100. It would quickly become a replicated and tangled web of symbolic and vector representations. Secondly, to achieve true knowledge reasoning, all architectures from the different data sources must somehow be communicating with each other. This is likely to cause catastrophic variations in both our knowledge base and knowledge reasoning. There are multiple considerations that you need to make. For example, how will you handle contradictory data points?

As such, the current mechanisms of the NSAI framework don't seem to consider the possibility of exploiting multiple data sources for enhanced performance. However, research efforts have been put into enabling this functionality. More notably, the PullNet (https://arxiv.org/abs/1904.09537) and GRAFT-Net (https://arxiv.org/abs/1809.00782) algorithms both provide a template on how the NN can extract answers from multiple data sources (in both cases, the network can either use textual data, a knowledge base, or both). Nevertheless, exploiting multiple sources of information remains a challenging and non-trivial task for NSAI systems.

Dynamic reasoning

Although the field of NSAI attempts to take the best of the symbolic and sub-symbolic AI worlds, one challenge from the symbolic AI sphere made its way into the paradigm of NSAI. If you recall, one of the biggest issues with symbolic AI is its complexity when it comes to updating the knowledge base with new information.

In NSAI, this process is still somewhat challenging. Especially in today's world, data and events move rapidly, resulting in data points dynamically changing over time. For example, the statement "the president of the United States of America is Donald Trump" would have been valid in 2020. Today, not so much. As such, an NSAI should define a way to mine new logical rules and update (almost in a self-correcting manner) its knowledge base. Although knowledge extraction through an NN should help this cause, ensuring dynamic reasoning is an area that requires further study.

Query understanding for knowledge reasoning

The user typically interacts with an NSAI system by providing a query as input and waits for the machine to provide an answer to that query. This property essentially means that the system needs to do the following:

- Decompose and understand the user's query
- Traverse the knowledge base to retrieve the correct answer

This creates two challenges. The first is the challenge for the NSAI system to understand the user's query, especially as query complexity increases. The second is the system's ability to retrieve the correct answer efficiently, especially as the search space also increases in complexity. We have already seen drastic improvements regarding this with the introduction of the CLEVRER dataset, where that NSAI was now more capable of handling even more complex queries, including counterfactual questions. Nonetheless, query complexity can be significantly increased in the real world with multiple chained questions or questions requiring deep knowledge and understanding. In the CLEVRER example that we discussed in *Chapter 5*, we saw how the NSAI architecture could reason on spatial information. An example of increased query complexity could be to reason about an additional dimension, such as time.

In conclusion, the field of NSAI is far from full maturity. Several challenges and limitations are currently present that must be addressed for NSAI to reach its full potential. The results achieved by NSAI highlight its potential to develop explainable and robust systems to solve real-world problems. Nevertheless, the current challenges faced by NSAI offer us the opportunity to further refine the NSAI paradigm, propelling it to new heights in the process. Following this, we will shift our focus to discussing the main NSAI research gaps at present.

Research gaps in neuro-symbolic computing

Although the field of NSAI has grown significantly in research interest and popularity, it is still maturing. NSAI is proving to be rather promising and is seeing major financial investment from strong research and technical institutions such as MIT and IBM. In this section, we will briefly highlight the future NSAI research direction and study avenues of interest:

- Standardized datasets and comprehensibility tests for benchmarking:

  Like the existing CLEVR and CLEVRER datasets, the domain of NSAI would benefit from common datasets that can be used to benchmark existing and new techniques. These standardized resources are critical for comparative research.

- Strategies for NN inference using symbolic propositions.

- More comparative evaluations on the NSAI paradigm to determine the best NN architecture to use.

- Context-aware semantics:

  Further investigation on how semantics can be constructed and influenced by the problem context.

- Further studies on NSAI evaluation strategies:

  As classification and regression problems have evaluation metrics, which metrics should we monitor to evaluate NSAI? For example, should we monitor the algorithms' performance decay as we reduce training data? Or maybe monitor their energy consumption? How can we reliably evaluate reasoning capabilities?

- Pre-trained models:

  Investigate strategies to save and load already trained NSAI architectures to use for similar problems.

- Analogical reasoning via transfer learning:

  Investigate how a pre-trained NSAI system on one domain can be fine-tuned and customized to solve another domain.

  Transfer learning is the process of taking an already trained NN and re-training its final layer to fit a new problem. It has had great success in the DL world, and it would be interesting to see NSAI transfer learning experiments.

- Online/incremental learning:

  Online learning is the process of training a model in a sequential step-by-step process as data becomes available. In online learning, the model is simultaneously predicting and learning; new data points coming in are used to update the model and improve its performance on future incoming data points.

In conclusion, addressing the research gaps highlighted in this section is crucial for advancing the field of NSAI and unlocking its full potential. These challenges offer exciting opportunities for researchers and practitioners to collaborate and innovate, and we look forward to seeing future developments in this field. We'll discuss these exciting topics in detail in *Chapter 9*.

Summary

With the current technological advancements, NSAI has high expectations to reach. So far, researchers are hinting at rather promising results achieved by NSAI. The field is still emerging and relatively niche, but its properties and inherent understanding present interesting opportunities for NSAI.

Throughout this chapter, we discussed some of the main benefits of NSAI, as highlighted by research so far. We saw how NSAI can achieve high performance with significantly few data points while being highly interpretable and transparent. Some challenges and limitations of its parent techniques, mainly those of symbolic AI, are somewhat evident in NSAI. Mainly, challenges revolve around the knowledge base and the symbolic integration with NN. We also discussed the future research direction of NSAI.

In the next chapter, we will discuss some real-life applications of NSAI in various businesses and industries.

7
Applications of Neuro-Symbolic AI

Neuro-symbolic AI (NSAI) has ignited a new hope in machine-enabled human-level reasoning. The NSAI paradigm is being widely adopted in both business and academia. The number of NSAI applications has been on a steady increase, especially throughout the last 2 years or so. Both the research and business industries appear to be reacting positively toward this emerging framework. Since 2019, Google Scholar has ranked over 3,000 works of literature focusing on NSAI and its applications. Throughout this time, we have witnessed the birth of various NSAI use cases from a diverse pool of industries. Business investment in NSAI is a vital feat to achieve. Besides promoting further academic advancement, a healthy number of technical use cases also enable us to study and better understand the implications imposed by NSAI and assess its outlook. Testing out the technology in the wild is the perfect strategy to observe performance and reliability outside the lab environment.

This chapter aims to solidify the NSAI paradigm by discussing its various applications in the real world. We will look at the different NSAI architectures from different perspectives, highlighting their respective benefits and pitfalls. The purpose of this chapter is two-fold. Firstly, this chapter wants to collect applications at the forefront of the NSAI paradigm and study their implementation details. This chapter also wants to inspire creativity in adopting this composite AI framework. NSAI remains relatively emerging and niche. Recently, we saw some strides in studying development standards and system design principles for NSAI frameworks. Despite this, this area is yet to mature. Therefore, this chapter is crucial to understanding how we can better exploit NSAI and shape it to fit our use cases.

This chapter will be structured slightly differently from the ones before it. We will discuss NSAI applications from three different but relevant and significant industries. We will attempt to structure each application in the following manner: the problem statement and definition, and then the role of NSAI in the application.

Ultimately, this chapter will go over the thought process and architectures involved in designing real-world NSAI systems, as well as explore potential use cases for NSAI.

We will cover the following use cases in this chapter:

- Health – computational drug repurposing
- Education – student strategy prediction
- Finance – bank loan risk assessment

> **Disclaimer**
> None of the authors of this book are affiliated with any of the works mentioned, nor their respective institutions.

Application 1 – health – computational drug repurposing

Statista (source: `https://www.statista.com/outlook/dmo/ecommerce/beauty-health-personal-household-care/health-care/worldwide`) shows that the worldwide healthcare domain is projected to generate revenue figures exceeding US$63 billion in 2023 while enjoying an annual growth rate of 10.15%. Numbers aside, the health domain is one of the few industries directly affecting everyone. Subsequently, its relevance to the average Joe is significant.

The health industry is not new to the field of AI. Several AI applications exist, from disease research acceleration to drug discovery, medical imaging, and patient screening. More recently, AI played a massive role in accelerating the discovery of the COVID-19 vaccine (see `https://sloanreview.mit.edu/audio/ai-and-the-covid-19-vaccine-modernas-dave-johnson/`). It is safe to say that the health domain motivates AI research. Given its extreme sensitivity, one of the biggest challenges faced by AI in health is its lack of interpretability (as discussed in *Chapter 4*).

There is currently a focus in the AI field on creating more transparent AI and being less reliant on complex mathematical concepts that can be difficult to understand. This is especially important when technical solutions need to be regulated. For example, the **Food and Drug Administration (FDA)** is trying to stop animal testing in favor of AI methods (refer to `https://www.nature.com/articles/d41586-022-03569-9`). The goal is for a more transparent AI that is also easier to comprehend. For this reason, NSAI is anticipated to advance the role of AI in healthcare drastically.

Application details

Drancé, M., Boudin, M., Mougin, F., and Diallo, G. (2021). *Neuro-symbolic XAI for Computational Drug Repurposing*. In Proceedings of the 13th International Joint Conference on Knowledge Discovery, Knowledge Engineering, and Knowledge Management – KEOD, ISBN 978-989-758-533-3; ISSN 2184-3228, pages 220-225. DOI: 10.5220/0010714100003064: `https://dl.acm.org/doi/abs/10.1007/978-3-031-00129-1_51`.

Problem statement

A 2019 study found that the average cost of developing a new drug is estimated to sit around the US$1.3 billion mark (source: `https://jamanetwork.com/journals/jama/fullarticle/2762311`) and likely involves several years of research and development. Billions of dollars are poured into drug research every single year. Due to this, this field of healthcare is rather attractive for researchers. The possible returns on investment stand to be significant while simultaneously influencing a tangible societal impact.

For this reason, drug repurposing has quickly become an exciting area of study for AI. Rather than researching for the discovery or development of an entirely new drug, the domain of drug repurposing is concerned with taking known and already studied drugs and applying them to newer diseases. This process is commonly referred to as linking, whereby we link an existing drug with a new application.

Deep learning techniques have been applied to link prediction in several instances. However, the consensus remains that AI should not be the decision-maker in these cases. Instead, AI should solely provide support to the medical expert and researcher. Machines cannot be held accountable, and in such critical applications, a human expert(s) must give the green light after extensive studies.

The role of NSAI

The rise of NSAI has been an exciting avenue for the drug repurposing field. The computational complexity and lack of interpretability presented by deep learning solutions meant that researchers could not rely on or trust the results of these algorithms. NSAI inspired researchers in this domain with new hope. Its transparent and explainable nature meant that the researchers could fully understand the link predictions and potentially backtrack the process and adjust.

The symbolic nature of NSAI meant that researchers could interact with the algorithm during the training process, supplying it with background knowledge through logical rules. Let's explore further how this was made possible through NSAI.

Understanding the data

This application's researchers used the OREGANO dataset (refer to `https://gitub.u-bordeaux.fr/erias/oregano/-/tree/oregano_app_4.0`). OREGANO is a **knowledge graph (KG)** built from multiple open data sources and specifically for biomedical research. It consists of over 360k nodes (11 distinct types, such as drugs, symptoms, and diseases) and over 800k relations (19 distinct types, such as `is_caused_by`, `associated_to`, and `is_substance_that_treats`). You can see its complete schema in *Figure 7.1*:

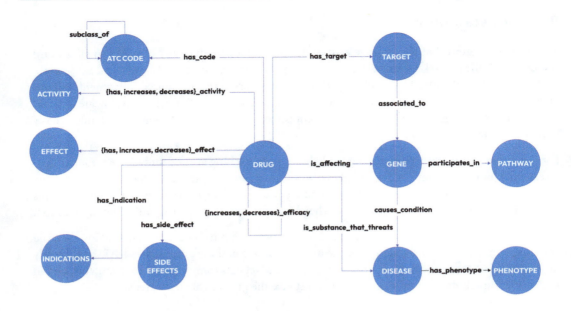

Figure 7.1: The OREGANO KG schema
(adapted from Drancé, M., Boudin, M., Mougin, F., and Diallo, G. (2021),
Neuro-symbolic XAI for Computational Drug Repurposing)

At its core, a KG is nothing more than a collection of symbols connected through relations. A KG maps its problem domain into a bunch of logical rules. This is perfect for satisfying the symbolic side of NSAI! One direct benefit of combining NSAI with KGs is the ease of extracting logical rules to integrate during training.

Considering the KG schema in *Figure 7.1*, we can start to identify how our logic propositions might look. The researchers in this study often refer to these rules as meta-paths (that is, the different paths you might take to eventually link two nodes, such as an existing molecule with another disease).

The structure of a meta-path might look something like this:

Figure 7.2: An example of a meta-path extracted from the OREGANO KG

The NSAI component

The NSAI framework implemented here involves combining a reinforcement learning algorithm (based on a **long short-term memory (LSTM)** network) and the logic rules encapsulated within the KG (in the form of meta-paths). One crucial aspect in extracting the meta-paths is that they should be represented as horn rules.

Defining horn rules

Named after the logician Alfred Horn, a horn rule is any clause that describes, at most, one positive literal.

Suppose we want to describe the current weather in logical form. It is currently raining, so we come up with a statement like *rain OR not sunny OR not snowing*. Our statement comprises three literals (*rain, sunny, and snowing*), out of which only one is positive (*rain*). Therefore, our statement is considered to be a horn clause. If we were to change the statement to *rain OR not sunny OR windy*, we would have more than one positive literal and fail to satisfy the property of the horn clause. Due to this characteristic, horn clauses are commonly described as the disjunction of literals. It is important to note that the statement "*not rain OR not windy OR not snowing*" (that is, all literals are negative) is also considered a horn clause and referred to as the goal clause.

By representing knowledge as horn clauses, it is possible to use automated reasoning algorithms to infer new knowledge or find contradictions. Horn clauses are thus an essential component of many AI and expert systems applications.

In addition to the horn clause representation, this NSAI framework requires every single logic rule that's extracted to be scored in terms of reliability. This scoring mechanism is essential during training when the reinforcement learning algorithm decides whether to punish or reward the individual prediction. The researchers opted to provide a reliability score ranging between 0 and 1 (0 representing poor, and 1 representing strong reliability).

The NSAI algorithm is called **Policy-guided walks with Logical Rules (PoLo)**, and its training process follows that of a **Markov Decision Process (MDP)**. MDP is a mathematical framework that enables computers to make decisions based on the probabilities of different things happening based on individual choices. The objective of PoLo is to find a reliable and successful linkage in drug repurposing. The process commences from an agent at an initial entity – usually a node representing a particular drug to be repurposed. Here, an agent is a worker or process that can execute several steps to move between different nodes. The agent aims to progress from one node to another until we reach another satisfactory entity (such as treating a disease or symptom). The agent can move to the next node or stay at the current node. This move is selected using a stochastic policy from the reinforcement learning algorithm. The extracted meta-paths are integrated with the training process through these stochastic policies. The entire travel history (called the chain of reasoning) between nodes is stored. This process is repeated until the agent receives a reward from the algorithm. The entire system can be seen in *Figure 7.3*:

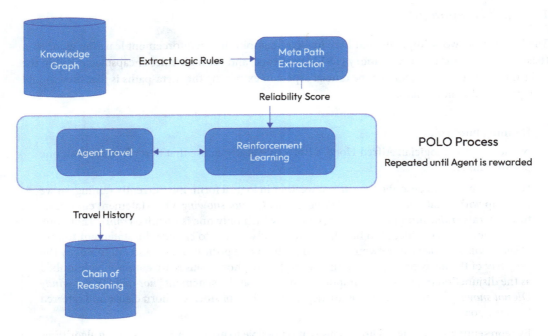

Figure 7.3: An overview of the NSAI architecture

The contribution of NSAI

Explainability is achieved through the chain of reasoning's transparency and the node traversal decision's interpretability. The NSAI framework described in this use case achieved comparable results to the state-of-the-art across several evaluation metrics. Using NSAI, the researchers developed a more interactive training process that was enhanced with explainable results at no sacrifice in performance.

Application 2 – education – student strategy prediction

The education sector is rapidly advancing and embracing new technologies to enhance the learning experience for students. AI is revolutionizing education by providing a more engaging, personalized learning experience for students. AI allows educators to tailor learning plans to each student's needs and abilities, leading to more effective and personalized instruction. By utilizing AI, educators can personalize instruction, provide real-time feedback, and analyze data to improve educational outcomes. Furthermore, AI can assist with administrative tasks such as grading and course planning, allowing teachers to focus on their primary role of instruction. By integrating AI into the education industry, we can expect improved student outcomes and increased efficiency in delivering education.

Application details

Shakya, A., Rus, V., and Venugopal, D. (2021). *Student Strategy Prediction Using a Neuro-Symbolic Approach*. International Educational Data Mining Society: `https://eric.ed.gov/?id=ED615630`.

Problem statement

At the core of this application are **Adaptive Instructional Systems (AISs)**. AISs are computer-based systems that can adjust (or, as the name implies, adapt) their content and learning material to meet the needs of the respective learner. Data and AI techniques often power these systems. They monitor student metrics such as time to answer to assess student performance. Every student is unique in their learning abilities, and understanding these styles will help ensure a more effective and engaging learning experience.

Nonetheless, matching students with their learning styles is not a trivial task. Multiple factors, including our expertise in the subject, level of interest or passion, and intellectual capacity, substantially influence how we learn. These factors all play a role in determining the most effective learning strategy. Ultimately, the main objective of an AIS is to understand the learning process of the individual student and their thought process when solving a task or problem.

The benefits of an AIS system become especially relevant in large learning settings. On a small dataset of pupils, a human expert might manage to extract student learning strategies. However, consider a school or university with thousands or even hundreds of thousands of students (for example, Indira Gandhi National Open University has more than four million students enrolled!). The manual process quickly becomes unfeasible, unscalable, and unrealistically expensive. Automating this process using AI systems ensures robustness, scalability, and consistency.

The role of NSAI

AIS has been predominantly implemented using **deep neural networks (DNNs)**. We have discussed the limitations of DNNs in *Chapters 3* and *5*, primarily their resource-hungry nature. Additionally, the researchers behind this application also note how DNNs are susceptible to overfitting, especially as we increase the datasets. The objective of NSAI here is simple: improve the generalization and scalability capabilities of DNN for AISs. Next, we will delve deeper into the NSAI solution behind this application.

Understanding the data

The primary datasets used for this application are the publicly available **KDD Education Data Mining (EDM)** datasets (see `https://pslcdatashop.web.cmu.edu/KDDCup/rules_data_format.jsp`). The dataset is in a *structured tabular* format and details the steps taken to solve a particular task (referred to as **knowledge component (KC)**) per student ID. Suppose we want to compute the area of a rectangle. First, we measure its length, then its width, and finally, multiply them to get the area. These three steps represent three KCs in the problem of calculating the area of a rectangle.

This data was collected by having students solve several KCs on a particular AIS. Also monitored per row is the number of hints a student uses at every step. One example where the AIS can ultimately adapt to provide a more tailored experience to the student is by anticipating at which steps the student would require more hints.

The NSAI component

The main objective of this use case is to aid in predicting the next instructional steps that a student is likely to follow. We can think of this problem as a sequencing task. The steps taken by a student to solve the problem are all connected, and one decision ultimately influences the other. In this application, we can see an NSAI architecture (shown in *Figure 7.4*) built on top of two popular sequencing techniques: **hidden Markov models** (**HMMs**) and DNN.

Regarding DNNs, LSTM is used to handle sequential data, where the order of the data points is essential. LSTMs are particularly useful for modeling if there are dependencies between data points spread over time. The critical feature of LSTMs is their ability to remember previous data points, allowing them to consider long-term dependencies. LSTMs accomplish this using a set of gates (input, forget, and output gates). These gates control the flow of information in and out of the network's hidden state. We discussed this type of network in greater detail in *Chapter 3*.

LSTMs have been used in many applications, such as language modeling, speech recognition, and time series forecasting. They have been proven more potent than traditional **recurrent neural networks** (**RNNs**) because they can handle longer-term dependencies in the data. Nonetheless, they also have more extensive parameters and require more computational resources to train. The latter is perhaps their most significant flaw, as noted by the researchers of this application. The larger the training data, the slower and more expensive it becomes.

Furthermore, in LSTMs, every observation in the dataset is considered **independent and identically distributed** (**IID**).

A brief segment on independent and identically distributed variables

Independent random variables are random variables that are not affected by the value of any other random variable. Therefore, their probability distribution does not depend on the value of any other random variable. For example, the roll of a fair die is independent of the roll of another fair die.

Identically distributed random variables are random variables that have the same probability distribution. This means that all the random variables have the same probability density function or probability mass function, regardless of the variable. For example, all the fair dice rolls have the same probability of getting a number between 1 and 6.

A sample is considered an IID if it is independent and identically distributed. This property is vital in many areas of statistics and probability as it allows us to make certain assumptions and simplify calculations. For example, in many statistical models, IID random variables represent the errors or noise in the data. Their IID property allows us to make assumptions about the distribution of the errors and use them for estimation and hypothesis testing.

The IID property in LSTMs is also partially problematic in this use case. The dataset records every single step in a student's problem-solving exercise. This results in having multiple related individual instances belonging to the same student and potentially even the same task (differing only in sub-task or KC). For example, the same student will likely adopt the same strategy to solve the same KC but a different problem.

The NSAI framework is a composite between Markov Logic (a symbolic program based on the Markov process) and an LSTM architecture. Markov Logic combines the representational power of first-order logic with probabilistic graphical models. The resultant graph is called the **Markov Logic Network (MLN)**. It allows for creating a knowledge base by combining a set of first-order logic formulas with a set of weight parameters. Every logic formula comprises two primary entities: a symbol and a relation.

This notation follows the symbolic logic structure we discussed in *Chapter 2*. A symbol represents an object (such as the student or the KC), while the relation specifies the logical connection between different objects. As such, the knowledge base in this application is constructed by extracting the domain logic encapsulated within the historical data in the form of first-order logic rules. Here is a trivial logic rule describing the relationship between a particular student and a problem:

$$STUDENT_{(S)} \land PROBLEM_{(P)} \Rightarrow KC_{(S,\ P,\ T)}$$

Here, S represents the student, P represents the problem, and T represents a particular step.

The knowledge base can then be represented as an MLN. This MLN represents the symbols as nodes in the graph, connected through their relations. *Figure 7.4* shows an example of an MLN describing the relationships between three different KCs and two problems. The MLN is constructed on first-order logic rules describing the relationships between KC1, KC2, KC3, P1, and P2 (where KC stands for knowledge component and P denotes a problem):

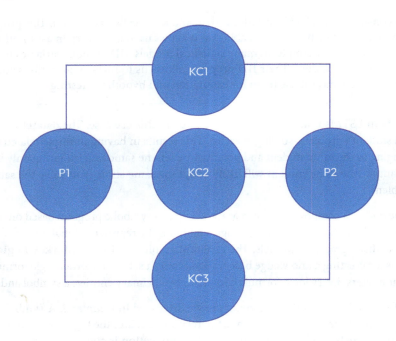

Figure 7.4: A simple MLN architecture

With the logical formula defined, we can use the weight parameter to determine the strength of the rules and how likely they are to be true. The researchers use these weights as part of a critical sampling strategy to filter essential student strategies. This application's NSAI architecture is different from the previous application.

Here, the primary purpose of the symbolic module is to improve the generalization and scalability performance of the LSTM rather than to augment the training process. This goal is achieved by using the extracted MLN to discover symmetrical student strategies (that is, homogenous strategies) and ultimately create a smaller subset of the dataset that retains the original dataset's information.

For instance, consider *Figure 7.4*. We can observe that both P1 and P2 are connected to nodes KC1, KC2, and KC3. Therefore, P1 and P2 are symmetric since they relate to the same KCs (that is, they can be solved through the same steps).

The researchers transform the student and problem logic rules from the MLN into their respective vector embeddings (using the Obj2Vec algorithm at `https://github.com/eangius/obj2vec`) and cluster them. The subset is created by taking random samples per cluster. The weight parameters discussed previously assign an importance weighting per cluster. This cluster importance weight determines the number of samples taken from every cluster (that is, the higher the cluster weight, the higher its student strategy rules' importance).

The objective here is to end up with different clusters of strategies with a high inter-cluster distance and a low intra-cluster separation. The result becomes a smaller dataset that drastically improves the efficiency of the training process.

The role of Markov Logic (and, as a result, the symbolic AI component from the NSAI framework) in this application is knowledge representation. The researchers finally trained a one-to-many LSTM model using the embedding vectors. These embeddings are one-hot-encoded and passed as inputs to the LSTM, and the model outputs a sequence of predicted KCs that students might follow to solve the respective problem. This NSAI architecture can be seen in *Figure 7.5*:

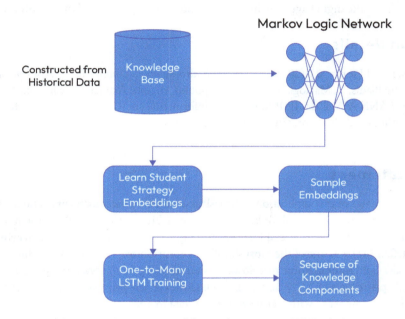

Figure 7.5: An overview of the student strategy NSAI solution

The contribution of NSAI

This NSAI architecture uses the symbolic AI component as a sub-sampling strategy to reduce the training set's size while retaining the same information. The symbolic rules do not actively interact with the training process and rather enable the resource-hungry LSTM network to train faster and more efficiently. The NSAI framework was evaluated and compared against two standalone solutions, one using HMM and the other a pure LSTM implementation. The NSAI approach outperformed both techniques and proved better in performance and scalability, all using a considerably smaller training dataset.

Application 3 – finance – bank loan risk assessment

In the ever-evolving world of finance, there is a growing need to stay ahead of the curve and be competitive. AI has proven to be a powerful tool in achieving this, providing financial institutions with real-time data processing, generating accurate predictions, and automating mundane and repetitive tasks. AI is not restricted to large financial organizations. Small and medium-sized companies can also exploit AI to provide valuable insights into operations and customer behavior. As regulations become increasingly complex and the threat of fraud looms, AI can also assist financial institutions in complying with regulations and detecting fraudulent activities. As the finance industry continues to evolve and adapt to the digital age, the importance and necessity of AI will only continue to grow.

Application details

Hatzilygeroudis, I. and Prentzas, J. (2011). *Fuzzy and Neuro-Symbolic Approaches to Assessment of Bank Loan Applicants.* In: Iliadis, L., Maglogiannis, I., Papadopoulos, H. (eds) Artificial Intelligence Applications and Innovations. EANN AIAI 2011. IFIP Advances in Information and Communication Technology, vol 364. Springer, Berlin, Heidelberg: `https://link.springer.com/chapter/10.1007/978-3-642-23960-1_10`.

Problem statement

The problem at the center of this application is the risk assessment of bank loan applications. Assessing the risk of a loan application is crucial for banks and financial institutions. It allows them to identify potential defaults and mitigate financial loss. Issuing high-risk bank home loans (carrying a high probability of defaulting) was one of the most significant contributors to the devasting financial crisis of 2008, which saw eight million home foreclosures (source: `https://www.newyorkfed.org/newsevents/speeches/2017/dud171106`). However, the process can be immensely time-consuming and labor-intensive, with a large volume of data to analyze.

Additionally, traditional risk assessment methods, such as credit scoring, may not fully capture the complexity and uncertainty of the loan application process. AI techniques can automate and improve the loan risk assessment process, reducing processing time and mitigating additional risk.

The role of NSAI

Support vector machines (**SVMs**) and genetic algorithms have been successfully employed in the bank loan risk assessment task. Due to its exceptional predictive abilities, there has also been a growing interest in using DNN for this purpose. Despite their effectiveness, a significant drawback of these algorithms is their lack of interpretability, making it difficult for bank loan officers to understand the reasoning behind the predictions. This lack of interpretability and the need for a more robust and capable system led the researchers to explore other approaches to this application.

One key aspect that's overlooked in traditional algorithms is integrating domain knowledge from experienced banking loan officers. These experts possess a wealth of domain logic that can be leveraged to improve the performance of the AI system. However, acquiring and incorporating this knowledge has traditionally been challenging, requiring extensive data manipulation and feature engineering. This approach increases the system's complexity and introduces the risk of human bias.

This paper presents two solutions: a fuzzy expert system and an NSAI expert system. In this section, we will focus on the latter, which aims to overcome the limitations of traditional algorithms by seamlessly integrating domain knowledge and providing interpretable and robust predictions.

Understanding the data

This problem presents two facades of looking at the task, which ultimately converge: the loan and personal sides. For a robust inferencing process, we must know about *who* (that is, the personal side) is applying for *which* (that is, the loan side) loan. The researchers described some of the monitored attributes. Here's a table of them:

Loan Attributes	• Type of Loan • Application Reason • Supporting Documents • Interest Details • Loan Amount • Loan Installment Types
Personal Attributes	• Net Annual Income • Overall Financial Status • Number of Dependencies (for example, children) • Age • Social Status

Table 7.1: Overview of the main attributes available in the dataset

The NSAI component

The basis of this NSAI system is neurules.

Defining neurules

A neurule is a hybrid AI system that combines neural networks and rule-based reasoning to make decisions. This approach allows a more flexible and adaptive system to learn from data and evolve.

Neurules use a neural network to learn patterns in data and use this knowledge to generate rules that can be used to make decisions. They are instrumental in applications such as natural language processing, computer vision, and decision-making, where the ability to handle complexity and uncertainty is required.

The symbolic component in neurules is given priority, and the neural network aspect is used primarily to improve the predictive performance. The neurules serve the purpose of knowledge base construction. This approach is advantageous because the knowledge base can retain the underlying structure and relationships of the production of symbolic rules. As we have discussed on several occasions, the main benefit of symbolic rules is their highly interpretable nature. The structure of neurules follows the symbolic rules (that is, in if-then-else format), rendering neurules to carry a robust interpretable property.

A neurule comprises one or more conditions, where every condition specifies a **significance factor** (**SF**). The purpose of the SF is to describe the condition's importance. The symbolic aspect of the neurules is based on the production rules, while the neural network component uses **adaptive linear units** (**ALUs**). The researchers formally define a condition in the following manner:

```
<condition> ::= <variable><predicate><value>
```

Here, the variable is any object or symbol within our knowledge base, the predicate can either be an equality or an inequality, and the value represents the parameter assigned to the variable.

Suppose we want to extract a neurule that describes what we wear based on the weather. We can have the following conditions (depicted using the C prefix), along with their respective SF (note that the SF values here are purely random and fictitious):

- C1: Going out is true (0.8)

- C2: The wind is not strong (0.5)

- C3: Precipitation > 0 mm (0.5)

An example neurule might look something like this:

```
IF
    C1 (0.8),
    C2 (0.5),
    C3 (0.5)
THEN
    BRING UMBRELLA
```

As we can see, the neurule structure is straightforward, transparent, and traceable. Every neurule is also assigned an "importance weight" parameter called the **bias factor** (**BF**). As a result, modeling a neurule as an ALU looks something like this:

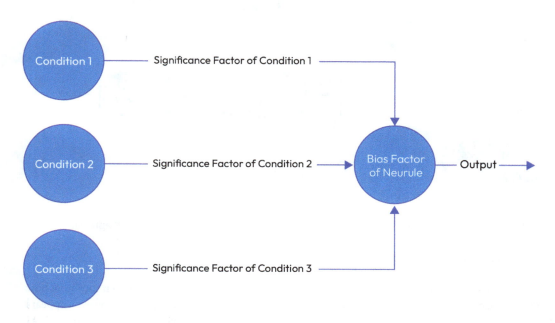

Figure 7.6: An example of an ALU representation of a simple neurule

Neurules are either extracted historically using the existing datasets or using empirical data (through training patterns). The extracted neurules are then stored in a neurule knowledge base. Similarly, the various loan details described in *Table 7.1* are stored in a separate knowledge base. The NSAI system communicates with both knowledge bases at inference. This process is repeated for every neurule extracted; thus, every single neurule becomes an ALU, as illustrated in *Figure 7.6*.

The inputs of the ALU are the actual conditions that make up the neurule. The input weights are defined using the condition's SF and the BF of the neurule. The researchers trained the ALU using the Least Mean Squares (refer to the *Further reading* section) algorithm.

The outputs in this application can either be 1 (*success*) or -1 (*failure*). Generating explanations is trivial. Given a decision, we can trace back the neurules and their BF, along with their respective conditions and SF. This entire process can be seen in *Figure 7.7*:

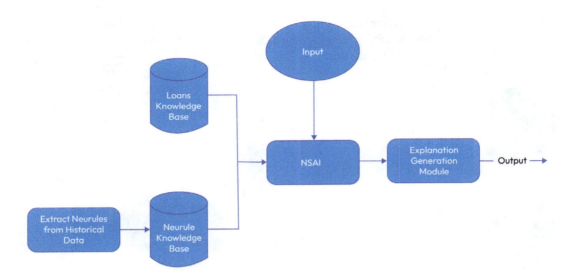

Figure 7.7: The logic flow of the NSAI framework for the "bank loan risk assessment" application

The contribution of NSAI

The researchers do not compare the results against other known benchmarks; however, they note how both approaches (the expert system and NSAI) seem to perform similarly. The NSAI, however, appears to be drastically more robust out of the two when we consider the sensitivity evaluation metric (NSAI obtained a score of 0.80 compared to the 0.66 achieved by the expert system).

Summary

Throughout this chapter, we highlighted the importance and potential of NSAI in various real-world applications. By combining the strengths of both neural networks and symbolic reasoning, NSAI can handle the complexity and uncertainty of real-world problems, providing valuable insights and accurate predictions. This chapter discussed using NSAI in the healthcare, education, and finance industries in separate applications.

This chapter showed how NSAI can help solve real-world problems. As AI continues to evolve, the use of NSAI will become increasingly important. The investigated applications show that NSAI is a powerful tool for solving complex problems and offers the added benefit of interpretability, which is essential for real-life applications. A common theme in these NSAI applications is that we obtain improved learning using fewer data points. Reusing the existing knowledge base also results in a more reliable and robust model. The different applications leverage the NSAI concept in varying and exciting ways and are inspired by different NSAI advantages.

In the healthcare example, we saw how we could leverage NSAI on graph structures. In this use case, symbolic rules in meta-paths are directly used to interact with the training process, influencing how the agent traverses the graph. The primary motivation behind this NSAI system was prediction explainability.

The education example presented an exciting twist to the NSAI architecture. In this case, symbolic AI was used as a knowledge reasoning and representation language on a tabular dataset. First-order logic rules were used to logically represent the knowledge base and generate an enhanced version of the training dataset (consisting of significantly fewer data samples that provide the same information gain as the original dataset). As such, the symbolic AI component does not directly interact with the LSTM model used for training. Instead, it is used as a data processing and training preparation strategy. In this application, we saw a different angle to NSAI. The researchers exploited the NSAI paradigm to train a model that can generalize and scale better.

Finally, in the finance application, we observed an NSAI system that seemed to be a mix of the other two applications. In this example, neurules were extracted from a historical relational data store. The neurules were based on symbolic production rules and were represented as ALUs. Here, training is done directly on the neurules. Here, we observed how NSAI helped achieve consistent predictive performance and explainability.

In the next chapter, we will build a simple NSAI system using the Python programming language.

Further reading

To learn more about the topics that were covered in this chapter, take a look at the following resources:

- PoLo NSAI algorithm: `https://arxiv.org/abs/2103.10367`
- Markov Logic Networks: `https://homes.cs.washington.edu/~pedrod/papers/mlj05.pdf`
- Adaptive linear units: `https://studyglance.in/nn/display.php?tno=5&topic=Adaptive-Linear-Neuron`
- Least Mean Squares: `https://danieltakeshi.github.io/2015-07-29-the-least-mean-squares-algorithm/`
- NSAI design principles: `https://link.springer.com/article/10.1007/s10489-021-02394-3`

8

Neuro-Symbolic Programming in Python

Neuro-symbolic artificial intelligence (**NSAI**) systems are not constrained by standardized principles or confined by special requirements. The only consideration in NSAI systems is the combination of symbolic **artificial intelligence** (**AI**) and **neural networks** (**NNs**). As reviewed in the previous chapter, NSAI implementations vary widely in scope and architecture. Although NSAI is a product of decades of research, the marriage between the two fields remains fresh. Some frameworks have gained more traction than others; however, none stand out as state of the art yet. Even evaluation strategies focused on NSAI algorithms are yet to solidify. Designing NSAI solutions requires solid creative direction by the developers, heavily influenced by domain knowledge and expertise. When working with NSAI, there are some considerations to keep in mind. How will deep learning interact (either directly or indirectly) with the symbolic learning component? How will we interpret the results of both components?

This chapter will provide a basic programmatic outline to design and implement NSAI systems using Python. In addition, the chapter will provide a fundamental reference point to extract symbolic logic and implement symbolic reasoning. This chapter is not intended to be a comprehensive guide to neuro-symbolic programming. Instead, we aim to instill a direction in aspiring developers looking to get started with NSAI. We will use a real dataset to discuss and implement two different NSAI solutions in Python.

The first objective of this chapter is to identify a strategy for designing and implementing an NSAI system. There are various ways to build such a system. In this chapter, we build a system based on the **logic tensor network** (**LTN**) architecture and another simple solution based on the prediction stacking of **decision trees** (**DTs**) and NNs. This architecture provides the necessary building blocks and thought process to understand how one should approach an NSAI system. Following, we will discuss how to represent data symbolically and integrate them with an NN in Python.

Ultimately, this chapter will go through the following topics:

- How to set up and prepare our environment for neuro-symbolic programming
- How to build a simple LTN
- How to build a simple NSAI architecture by exploiting DTs to extract symbolic representations

Environment and data setup

The main objective of this chapter is to introduce the different mechanisms and thought processes associated with neuro-symbolic programming. This chapter is not designed as a programming crash course for symbolic or deep learning. For this purpose, we will work with the *Red and White Wine Dataset* (`https://www.kaggle.com/datasets/numberswithkartik/red-white-wine-dataset`) – publicly available in Kaggle. This dataset consists of 12 features describing different wine characteristics (such as the density and residual sugar, to name a couple) and a binary label representing whether said wine is a `red` or `white` wine. Some characteristics that made this dataset ideal for our use case were the following:

- It has around 6,000 samples, making it ideal for showing the power of NSAI by varying the size of the training data

- It does not require much data pre-processing or engineering

- It is a standard binary classification task, making it more straightforward to frame and structure

As our development environment, we will use the Google Colaboratory (Colab) platform (`https://colab.research.google.com/`). Given the small dataset, we do not require GPUs to distribute deep learning training. As a result, the following can easily be reproduced locally using the average personal computer. We opt for Colab to facilitate setting up the Python environment. You can find the Jupyter notebook and the dataset in the book's official GitHub repository: `https://github.com/PacktPublishing/Neuro-Symbolic-AI`.

We can download the dataset from Kaggle and upload it to the Colab session. Then, we load the dataset directly into Python using the pandas package in a variable called `df`:

```
import pandas as pd
df = pd.read_csv('/content/wine_dataset.csv')
```

We notice an extra column, `quality`, part of our DataFrame. This column is another independent variable (i.e., label) that we can predict. For the purpose of this example, we will focus on the `style` column as our label. We can call the `drop()` function to remove a column from the DataFrame (by passing the `axis=1` parameter). We perform this operation *in place*, which is performed on the DataFrame itself rather than returning a new DataFrame object. We can perform this operation as follows:

```
df.drop('quality', axis=1, inplace=True)
```

We also need to transform our `style` label to either `True` or `False` to represent whether the wine is a red wine or not. We can do this as follows:

```
df['style'] = np.where(df['style'] == 'red', True, False)
```

On inspection, it seems that our samples are sorted by their label. So, to get some randomness going, we can shuffle the dataset. One way to do this operation is to take a sample from the DataFrame equal to 100% of its size (to get all rows available). To do this, we can use the `sample()` function and pass in 1 as our `frac` parameter. The `frac` parameter specifies the percentage of the dataset we want to return.

```
df = df.sample(frac=1)
```

We have successfully loaded the dataset in Python and can build our NSAI solution.

Solution 1 – logic tensor networks

In our first Python NSAI example, we will implement a system based on the **Logic Tensor Network (LTN)** framework.

In short, LTNs are a sub-class of neural networks that leverage logical propositions (i.e., symbolic logic). LTNs use logical propositions to represent the knowledge base as formulas and deep learning to learn the different weights of these formulas. These logical propositions act as soft constraints on the neural network's inference. If the neural network's output violates the logical propositions, then it is penalized. As a result, an LTN during training has two main objectives: 1) satisfy the logical propositions, and 2) improve its predictive performance on the target objective. As such, the logical propositions as model constraints act as a way to directly integrate prior domain knowledge into the neural network.

For the more interested reader, you can read the full LTN paper at `https://arxiv.org/pdf/1606.04422.pdf`.

The first objective is, therefore, to correctly represent our dataset (i.e., the knowledge base) as logical formulas. In LTNs, we typically represent these logical formulas as axioms.

Defining an axiom

An axiom is a logical statement that is the general (and accepted) truth. Axioms are typically taken to be true without any proof and should be simple enough to be self-evident. Axioms can comprise connectives, predicates, terms, or propositions (or a mix).

For example, "if you add zero to any number, the result is always that same number" is an axiom.

We use these axioms to build a vector space of knowledge (i.e., we extend the first-order logical statements by representing them as multi-dimension vectors – from logical statements to tensors). We refer to this concept as *grounding*. The motivation behind the vector space representation is to enable relationship mapping and reasoning between the different logical statements, as opposed to *True* or *False* values supported by the axioms. This process is called *real logic* and is the core concept of LTNs.

In this chapter, we do not define or discuss the formal mathematical definitions of LTNs. Additionally, we will use the excellent Python library *LTNtorch* (`https://github.com/tommasocarraro/LTNtorch`). *LTNtorch* is an LTN implementation based on the deep learning package *PyTorch* (`https://github.com/pytorch/pytorch`). *LTNtorch* also comprehensively explains the mathematical foundations around the LTN algorithm.

Loading the dataset

First things first, let us install this package in our environment. In Colab, we can use the `!` operator to directly execute terminal commands from within the Python cell, as follows:

```
!pip install LTNtorch
```

Next, we want to import the required libraries. In this example, we need the following packages:

```
import torch
import ltn
import numpy as np
from sklearn.metrics import accuracy_score
```

At this point, we have already loaded our dataset. The remaining step is to split the dataset into features and labels and then split them into training and testing sets. For now, let us split the features:

```
features = df.drop('Class_att', axis=1).values
```

We will also standardize our features to have a zero mean and unit variance (i.e., a variance equal to 1). This step has several benefits. Mainly to remove scale influence (for example, the disparity between a feature measuring a person's age and another calculating their salary) and to help the NN converge faster (i.e., faster training). We use the following equation to perform this step:

$$x = \frac{x - \bar{x}}{\sigma}$$

Where x denotes the observation, $\bar{x}$ denotes the sample mean of x, and σ denotes the sample standard deviation of x:

```
# standardize our features
features = (features - features.mean()) / features.std()
```

Modifying the dataset

We will now split the labels and transform both features and labels into tensors directly using the *PyTorch* library. Again, we simply drop our label column (i.e., `style`) for our feature set. This time, we do not want the operation to be done *in place*. Instead, we want to return a new DataFrame. If we did this operation in place, then we would be overwriting our original DataFrame and therefore losing our `label` column. We call the `.values` property to return a NumPy representation of the DataFrame.

We load both features and labels as *PyTorch* tensors by calling the `torch.tensor()` function. We use the `.to()` function to specify the data type of our tensors:

```
# convert our features and labels to tensors
features = torch.tensor(features).to(dtype=torch.float32)
labels = torch.tensor(df['style'].values).to(dtype=torch.float32)
```

Creating train and test datasets

We'll now create our training and testing sets. We'll use *PyTorch's DataLoader* functionality to do so. The *DataLoader* allows us to pass batches of the dataset to our NN. We'll define a standard *PyTorch* DataLoader (read more at `https://pytorch.org/docs/stable/data.html#torch.utils.data.DataLoader`).

We create the class structure using the following:

```
class DataLoader(object):
```

The above `DataLoader` class must define three main functions:

`__init__`: The constructor for the class. It describes the different properties that every instance of that class can have. The main properties we are after are the data (i.e., our features), the labels, the batch size, and whether we want to shuffle the samples. We can implement it as follows:

```
def __init__(self, data, labels, batch_size=1, shuffle=True):
    self.data = data
    self.labels = labels
    self.batch_size = batch_size
    self.shuffle = shuffle
```

`__len__`: Logic to execute whenever we call the `len()` function on any instance of this class. This definition helps us determine the number of batches based on a specified batch size.

We divide the total number of samples (obtained using `.shape[0]`) by the specified batch size. We take the result's `ceil` (i.e., round up to the nearest integer value) as our total number of batches. This function looks like this:

```
def __len__(self):
    return int(np.ceil(self.data.shape[0] / self.batch_size))
```

`__iter__`: Describes the logic to run when we iterate over any instance of this class. This function is also used throughout the batching process.

This function needs to be an iterator. Based on our batch size, it should yield a series of batches from our features and labels. When creating our batches, keeping the number of samples from the different labels as balanced as possible is vital. For example, we only have two labels in our binary classification task. Therefore, we first separate and shuffle our samples based on their label:

```python
def __iter__(self):
    n = self.data.shape[0]
    idx_pos = np.where(self.labels == 1)[0]
    idx_neg = np.where(self.labels == 0)[0]
    np.random.shuffle(idx_pos)
    np.random.shuffle(idx_neg)
```

Then, we choose an equal (or fewer if there are not enough samples) subset of samples from both labels randomly per batch:

```python
for start_idx in range(0, n, self.batch_size):
    end_idx = min(start_idx + self.batch_size, n)

    # Get one positive and one negative sample for each batch
    pos_batch_size = min(self.batch_size // 2, len(idx_pos))
    neg_batch_size = self.batch_size - pos_batch_size
    pos_idx = idx_pos[:pos_batch_size]
    neg_idx = np.random.choice(idx_neg, size=neg_batch_size,
                               replace=False)
```

Finally, we concatenate the results, reshuffle them, and produce the features and labels for that batch:

```python
    idx = np.concatenate([pos_idx, neg_idx])
    np.random.shuffle(idx)

    data = self.data[idx]
    labels = self.labels[idx]
    yield data, labels
```

We take the first 91 samples as part of our training set and the remaining for testing. There is no specific reasoning behind the decision to take the first 91 samples for training. One can experiment with different percentage allocations between the training and testing sets. We restrict the training set to such a small amount to highlight the power of NSAI when it comes to small data. Of course, in the real world, it would be ideal to use all the data in our possession:

```python
# create training and testing dataloader, batch_size = 64
train_loader = DataLoader(features[:91], labels[:91], 64, True)
test_loader = DataLoader(features[91:], labels[91:], 64, False)
```

Defining our knowledge base and NN architecture

The next step is to extract the knowledge base (axioms) and create our NN. We define our predicate, the connectives, and the quantifiers.

> **Giving context to predicates, connectives, and quantifiers**
>
> **Predicate**: In LTNs, an algorithm maps a high-dimensional vector space to a specific label set. Our binary classification task requires the predicate to map to either 0 or 1.
>
> **Connective**: A logical connective such as a conjunction (*AND*), disjunction (*OR*), negation (*NOT*), or implication (*IMPLIES*).
>
> **Quantifier**: Describes how many (i.e., the quantity) samples satisfy the predicate. The two main quantifiers are *Universal* (indicates the *for all* amount, represented by the symbol ∀) and *Existential* (indicates the *exists* quantity, represented by the symbol ∃).

For our example, we define our predicate as a simple feed-forward NN using *PyTorch* (refer to *Figure 8.1*). We create a network with an input layer translating the dataset's 11 features to 64 neurons, a hidden layer with 64 neurons, and an output layer converging to a single neuron.

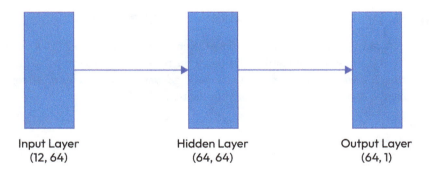

Input Layer
(12, 64)

Hidden Layer
(64, 64)

Output Layer
(64, 1)

Figure 8.1: The architecture used for our simple feed-forward NN

The network hyperparameter tuning procedure includes choosing the number of neurons per layer, which is often a trial-and-error process. We use the **Rectified Linear Unit** (**ReLU**) function to activate the input and hidden layers and the sigmoid function to limit the output of the output layer to the [0, 1] range. This is a standard architecture for most binary classification tasks:

```
# we define predicate A
class ModelA(torch.nn.Module):
    def __init__(self):
        super(ModelA, self).__init__()
        self.sigmoid = torch.nn.Sigmoid()
```

```
        self.layer1 = torch.nn.Linear(11, 64)
        self.layer2 = torch.nn.Linear(64, 64)
        self.layer3 = torch.nn.Linear(64, 1)

        self.relu = torch.nn.ReLU()
        self.dropout = torch.nn.Dropout(p=0.1)

    def forward(self, x):
        x = self.relu(self.layer1(x))
        x = self.relu(self.layer2(x))
        x = self.dropout(x)
        return self.sigmoid(self.layer3(x))
```

We keep the NN implementation simple for the sake of explanation. Moreover, our dataset is tiny, making it easy to overfit (i.e., the model fit is too close to the training data – essentially it would perform very well during training but significantly worse on unseen data) with unnecessarily complex networks. The predicate function (i.e., our deep learning component) would likely become increasingly difficult with more complex data structures and knowledge bases. One might also experiment with different NN architectures, for example, a convolutional NN (CNN).

Defining our predicate, connectives, and quantifiers

Next, we define our connectives and quantifiers. Implementing these is easy in *LTNtorch*. We define a *NOT* connective and a *FOR ALL* quantifier. These are the recommended settings by *LTNtorch* for binary classification. It is wise to dive deeper into the package's various options for more complex use cases to determine the correct configuration for your dataset:

```
# create our predicate (i.e., our NN)
A = ltn.Predicate(ModelA())

# create the NOT standard connective
Not = ltn.Connective(ltn.fuzzy_ops.NotStandard())

# create the FOR ALL quantifier
Forall = ltn.Quantifier(ltn.fuzzy_ops.AggregPMeanError(p=2),
                        quantifier="f")
```

We define the *FOR ALL* quantifier by specifying the quantifier parameter as f.

Here, the connective module contributes to the knowledge-base extraction by amalgamating sub-formulas with different features. The quantifier module determines the formula dimensions for tensor aggregation.

We are almost there!

Setting up evaluation parameters

Before we can train our LTN, we need a way to evaluate our system. We need to evaluate two aspects of the architecture.

The knowledge-base satisfaction level (the SAT level)

This metric answers the question of how good the LTN is at learning. We will use this throughout the training process as part of our loss function (we want to maximize this metric).

We can iterate over our data samples and split them based on their label. Then, per the label, we can compute the SAT level using the `SatAgg` function provided by LTNtorch by comparing the true samples with the predicted results from our NN:

```
def compute_sat_level(loader):
    mean_sat = 0
    for data, labels in loader:
        # get our positive samples
        x_A = ltn.Variable("x_A",data[torch.nonzero(labels)])
        # get our negative samples
        x_not_A = ltn.Variable("x_not_A", data[torch.nonzero(
                                    torch.logical_not(labels))])
```

Finally, we take the mean of the two SAT levels and repeat until we iterate over all samples:

```
        # get the mean SAT of both sample types
        mean_sat += SatAgg(Forall(x_A, A(x_A)),
                           Forall(x_not_A, Not(A(x_not_A)))
        )

    # get the mean SAT over all samples
    mean_sat /= len(loader)
    return mean_sat
```

The classification performance

This metric gives the overall performance of the model.

For our simple example, we will use the accuracy score implemented by sklearn (read more at https://scikit-learn.org/stable/modules/model_evaluation.html#accuracy-score). Depending on the use case, you might want to monitor one or more different metrics.

We iterate over all samples and measure the mean accuracy score by comparing the true labels and their respective predicted labels:

```
def compute_accuracy(loader):
    mean_accuracy = 0.0
    # iterate over our data samples
    for data, labels in loader:
        # get the predictions for the given samples
        predictions = A.model(data).detach().numpy()

        # convert to a binary classification (i.e., 0 or 1)
        predictions = np.where(predictions > 0.5, 1., 0.).flatten()

        # compute the accuracy_score
        mean_accuracy += accuracy_score(labels, predictions)
    # get the mean accuracy
    return mean_accuracy / len(loader)
```

We must also initialize a `SatAgg` object from the *LTNtorch* package to aggregate the SAT levels. At this step, we can also define the optimizer for our NN. We will use the standard Adam optimizer with a learning rate of 0.001. The Adam optimizer is an algorithm that optimizes the stochastic gradient descent process. In short, it is used to adjust the learning rate of NN throughout the training process:

```
SatAgg = ltn.fuzzy_ops.SatAgg()
optimizer = torch.optim.Adam(A.parameters(), lr=0.001)
```

Now, we are ready to train our LTN.

Training the LTN model

The training process is split as follows. First, we will start batching the data we created earlier for a certain number of epochs (i.e., iterations):

```
EPOCHS: int = 100
for epoch in range(EPOCHS):
    # reset the training loss for every epoch
    train_loss = 0.0

    # start batching the data
    for batch_idx, (data, labels) in enumerate(train_loader):
```

Per batch, we split the positive and negative samples into their respective variables and measure their individual SAT level using the created *FOR ALL* quantifier. We also need to call the `zero_grad()` function to set the gradients to zero before starting the backpropagation of the training process. This step is a standard process in the PyTorch library (to know more, you can have a look at this well-formulated Stack Overflow answer `https://stackoverflow.com/a/48009142/4587043`):

```
optimizer.zero_grad()

# we ground the variables with current batch data
x_A = ltn.Variable("x_A", data[torch.nonzero(labels)])
# positive examples
x_not_A = ltn.Variable("x_not_A", data[torch.nonzero(
                    torch.logical_not(labels))])
# negative examples


# compute SAT level
sat_agg = SatAgg(Forall(x_A, A(x_A)),
                 Forall(x_not_A, Not(A(x_not_A)))
)
```

Then, we calculate our loss value (by subtracting the computed SAT level from 1) and train the NN using back-propagation. This step helps us monitor the error margin in our SAT predictions. The smaller the loss value, the better our NN is performing. As such, we want to optimize learning by minimizing the loss value:

```
# compute loss and perform back-propagation
loss = 1. - sat_agg
loss.backward()
optimizer.step()
train_loss += loss.item()
```

After iterating over all batches, we monitor the current training loss and print to console the current results on every 20th epoch:

```
# monitor the training loss
train_loss = train_loss / len(train_loader)

# we print metrics every 20 epochs of training
if epoch % 20 == 0:
    print(" epoch %d | loss %.4f | Train Sat %.3f | Test Sat %.3f
| Train Acc %.3f | Test Acc %.3f"
        %(epoch, train_loss,
            compute_sat_level(train_loader),
            compute_sat_level(test_loader),
            compute_accuracy(train_loader),
            compute_accuracy(test_loader)))
```

Analyzing the results

Monitoring the training process, the SAT and accuracy scores improve with every epoch.

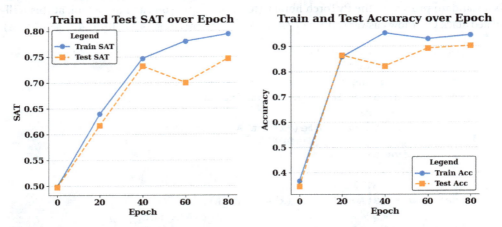

Figure 8.2: Train and test SAT (left) and accuracy (right) scores over the epochs

The preceding plots highlight an exciting benefit of LTNs, which we have already discussed in the previous chapters. The NSAI architecture generalizes quickly and arguably better (i.e., the model's performance on the unseen data is improved), resulting in a rapid training process. After 80 epochs, we reached an accuracy score of around 90% on the test set. However, after just 20 epochs, we got an accuracy figure of approximately 87% (starting at just under 35% at epoch 0). Considering that our training dataset consists of only 91 samples, this highlights the power of NSAI to achieve high performance with small data. The influence of LTNs in obtaining such predictive performance is also worth noting, with the only training objective being knowledge satisfaction. Including prior knowledge in training therefore improves the model's fit – especially in unseen cases. If we were to run the same training process using a training set of 5,000 samples (around 75% of the entire dataset), our results wouldn't vary too much. After 80 epochs, we obtain a testing accuracy score of around 92.3% (at the 20th epoch, we were already at 91.7%). Although increasing the number of training data samples did improve our model's performance, we must appreciate the performance obtained with training on just 91 random samples. Out in the real world, this difference in training sizes might translate to millions of dollars saved from overheads to see the entire training process through.

Granted, this task is a straightforward one and others have easily obtained 99% accuracy. However, if we compare these results against other documented ones, we can quickly start to appreciate the NSAI benefit of needing significantly smaller data to learn and less complex NN architectures. A similar experiment to ours based on NNs (https://www.kaggle.com/code/hhp07022000/wine-quality-prediction-and-type-classification) reached 99% accuracy after training for 700 epochs. It is also worth noting that the NN used in this experiment had double the size (with 128 neurons in the hidden layer compared to our 64). On larger-scale projects, these implications will have a significant value.

Another benefit of LTNs (and subsequently, NSAI) is their high transparency. We have stated multiple times that NSAI systems are explainable by default. The LTN training process involves translating first-order logic to tensor embeddings. We start off with logical relationships between variables and predicates. Then, we use quantifiers over the variables and predicates (returning either `True` or `False`) and transform them into multi-dimensional vectors (using tensor operations). As such, the resulting tensors embed the logical relationships. We can trace the entire process for every prediction by examining the tensor operations and logical connections.

Of course, out in the real world, the process would not be complete here. Instead, it typically involves a lot of back-and-forth experimenting with different hyperparameters to minimize over-fitting and improve model robustness.

Solution 2 – prediction stacking

We started this chapter by stating that NSAI is not constrained by design, development rules, or principles. It is simply the marriage of symbolic learning and NNs. What does this mean for us? First, we can still leverage the power of NSAI without using complex algorithms or spending too much time figuring out the best way to extract the knowledge base. NSAI is highly creative. Following, we will go through the process of implementing a much simpler NSAI system using the same dataset.

In our previous example, we focused on representing knowledge as axioms. We feed this representation to the NN to map the relationships between the various dimensions to learn knowledge. Another way to extract knowledge in the form of symbolic statements would be to use **decision trees** (**DTs**). DTs use logical rules to make decisions and map the training data in a tree-like structure. Every node in the tree represents some logical condition, and the subsequent nodes branch out from that node based on their relationship to that logical condition (i.e., whether they conform to it or not). Therefore, using a DT is an effective way to learn the underlying relationships of a task and extract its knowledge as logical conditions.

We can then combine the predictions obtained by the DT and stack them on top of those generated by the NN. Stacking means combining all predictions from both techniques and performing an aggregation. In Python, we can achieve this in just five lines of code.

Experiment setup and loading the data

We will be using the *scikit-learn* Python package to get this done. Let us start by importing the required functions into our environment:

```
from sklearn.model_selection import train_test_split
from sklearn.tree import DecisionTreeClassifier
from sklearn.neural_network import MLPClassifier
from sklearn.ensemble import StackingClassifier
```

We can now load it into our dataset and prepare it for modeling. This step is like our previous example, except for loading our data as tensors:

```
df = pd.read_csv('/content/wine_dataset.csv')
df.drop('quality', axis=1, inplace=True)
df['style'] = np.where(df['style'] == 'red', True, False)
df = df.sample(frac=1)
features = df.drop('style', axis=1)
features = (features - features.mean()) / features.std()
labels = df['style']
```

Data preparation

The next step is to split our features and labels into training and testing datasets. We can use the `train_test_split` function from sklearn, which automatically splits our data into training features, testing features, training labels, and testing labels. First, we specify a `test_size` of 0.2 to indicate that we want 80% of our data to contribute towards the training set and the remaining 20% to form our testing set. Note, this time around we are not restricting our training dataset to a few samples. Next, we set `random_state` to 42. This variable controls our seed parameter, and using the same number throughout our experiment ensures reproducible experiments (by consistently generating the same sequence of random numbers):

```
X_train, X_test, y_train, y_test = train_test_split(
    features, labels, test_size=0.2, random_state=42)
```

Training our NSAI model

Now, we can start building our simple NSAI system.

We first create a DT and a NN (this time using the sklearn package instead of PyTorch):

```
dt = DecisionTreeClassifier(random_state=42)
nn = MLPClassifier(hidden_layer_sizes=(64,), random_state=42)
```

Then, we need to define our stacking classifier. We will set the DT as the base estimator for the stacking classifier and the NN as the final estimator:

```
estimators = [('dt', dt), ('nn', nn)]
stacking_clf = StackingClassifier(estimators=estimators,
                                  final_estimator=nn)
```

The final step is to train the model by calling the `fit()` function. We pass our training features and labels to this function:

```
stacking_clf.fit(X_train, y_train)
```

Analyzing the results

We now have a fully trained NSAI system based on a stacking classifier. We can calculate the accuracy of our model as follows:

```
print(f"Accuracy: {stacking_clf.score(X_test, y_test):.3f}")
```

In our experiment, this approach returned an accuracy score of 99.4%. Different problems and use cases often require different strategies with varying levels of complexity to reliably solve them. We show this example to highlight that the power of NSAI lies not within the complexity of the approach but in the application of the core concepts. Although this simple architecture might not provide the required predictive power to handle complex tasks such as computer vision and natural language, it can be powerful for use cases with tabular data.

Prediction interpretability and logic tracing

Interpreting the results of this architecture is relatively straightforward. The role of the DT in this example is to extract the knowledge base in the form of logical rules. Thus, we can access the extracted rules directly from the DT, as follows:

```
from sklearn.tree import export_text

# Get the decision tree classifier from the stacking classifier
dt_clf = stacking_clf.estimators_[0]

# Convert the decision tree to rules using export_text
tree_rules = export_text(dt_clf,
                         feature_names=X_train.columns.tolist())

# Parse the text representation of the rules to create a list of rules
rule_list = [rule.strip() for rule in tree_rules.split('\n') if
             rule.strip()]
```

If we print the `rule_list`, we can get a full representation of the extracted knowledge base. Alternatively, using the `graphviz` package, we can visualize the entire tree as follows:

```
from sklearn.tree import export_graphviz
import graphviz

# Export the decision tree as a Graphviz file
```

```
dot_data = export_graphviz(dt_clf, out_file=None,
                           feature_names=X_train.columns,
                           class_names=['0', '1'],
                           filled=True, rounded=True,
                           special_characters=True)
graph = graphviz.Source(dot_data)

# Show the decision tree
graph
```

Here, in *Figure 8.3*, we show a small part of the full DT for illustration purposes. We can observe the different splits (i.e., the decisions) involved in classifying a sample. At every decision node, we can see the actual decision condition, the Gini index (measures the split's quality), the number of samples and values that satisfy that condition, and its class.

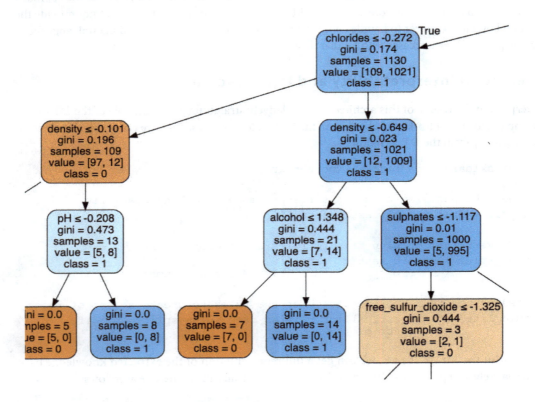

Figure 8.3: A small snippet of the resultant decision tree

Summary

We started this chapter by discussing the thought process behind developing an NSAI solution based on the powerful technique of LTNs. Then, we saw how LTNs combine symbolic rules and NNs to learn the relationships between the different logical conditions and their variables (i.e., the knowledge base). Thanks to the powerful *LTNtorch* package, we demonstrated how to quickly build an LTN system for a binary classification task. For example, we used the publicly available *Red and White Wine Dataset*. We showed the power and benefits of NSAI (specifically, LTNs) in training performance. Our LTN system reached high predictive power much quicker when compared to other public experiments on the same dataset.

In this chapter, we also discussed a more straightforward approach to NSAI. In this example, we directly combined a DT (as the symbolic AI component) and an NN as a stacking classifier. We showed how we can exploit the logic extraction capabilities of the DT to further understand the reasoning behind our predictions.

All in all, this chapter is intended to inspire creative thinking in developing NSAI solutions. There is not a single correct approach. At the end of the day, NSAI is about exploiting the interpretable power of symbolic representations and combining it with the predictive power of NNs.

NSAI is not the only emerging concept in the realm of AI. In the next chapter, we provide an outlook on the future of AI and the role that NSAI plays in it.

Further reading

You can check out the following resources to complement the topics discussed in this chapter:

- CNN-based Logic Tensor Network Application: `https://arxiv.org/abs/2103.09044`

- Introduction to deep learning: `https://www.analyticsvidhya.com/blog/2018/10/introduction-neural-networks-deep-learning/`

- LTNtorch tutorial on grounding and connectives: `https://github.com/tommasocarraro/LTNtorch/blob/main/tutorials/2-grounding_connectives.ipynb`

9
The Future of AI

I'm sure that by now, no one is doubting that **artificial intelligence (AI)** is one of the most powerful technologies of our time. It has enabled breakthroughs in many domains, including computer vision, natural language processing, speech recognition, self-driving cars, and more. But the million-dollar question is, what does the future hold? How will it impact our society, economy, and environment? What are the opportunities and challenges that lie ahead?

Top experts have different viewpoints on the matter.

Geoffrey Hinton, one of the pioneers of deep learning, believes that we need to go beyond the current paradigm of neural networks and explore new ways of modeling complex phenomena, such as causality, common sense reasoning, and consciousness. Recently, Geoffrey Hinton resigned from his position at Google over growing concerns about the ethical implications of AI.

Yoshua Bengio, another deep learning pioneer, is excited about generative AI models that can create realistic content, such as images, sounds, text, and videos. According to him, these models can help us understand human creativity and imagination. However, we have to be careful because even though their results are impressive, the technology behind them is not a step forward for AI research. The reason is that these models often rely on vast amounts of data and computational power rather than advanced algorithms, which may not lead to a deeper understanding of the underlying principles of human cognition.

Noam Chomsky, a renowned linguist and philosopher, has expressed concern about the prevalent and trendy approach to AI. In particular, he is referring to machine learning and its potential to negatively impact scientific progress and undermine ethical principles by integrating a fundamentally flawed understanding of language and knowledge into our technology. Chomsky argues that machine learning programs, such as ChatGPT, operate in a manner that is fundamentally different from human reasoning and language use. These disparities impose significant limitations on the capabilities of such programs.

Gary Marcus, a cognitive scientist and professor affiliated with **New York University** (**NYU**), has delved into the implications of large language models, such as OpenAI's GPT-3, for understanding the intricacies of the human mind. However, he has also expressed concerns about the potential exploitation of AI technology by nefarious individuals. To address this, Marcus proposes the establishment of a global organization tasked with overseeing and directing the development and deployment of AI systems.

Fei-Fei Li, a professor at Stanford University and a co-director of the Stanford **Human-Centered AI** (**HAI**) institute, is passionate about making AI better for humanity. She advocates for human-centered AI that respects diversity, fairness, privacy, and social good. She also involves humans in designing, developing, and deploying AI systems.

These are, of course, just a selection of views from global experts but they give us an insight into what we're going to explore. In this chapter, we will examine some of the most ambitious and controversial visions for AI, such as quantum computing and **artificial general intelligence** (**AGI**), as well as singularity. We will explain these terms, why they are essential, and how they might affect our world. In summary, this chapter aims to provide a broad overview of AI's future direction.

By the end of this chapter, you will have gained a comprehensive understanding of the most advanced AI research currently being conducted in labs. You will also get a glimpse into future research directions and delve into far-reaching developments in AI, such as AGI and singularity, by exploring their potential implications and their impact on our world.

Specifically, we will cover the following topics in this chapter:

- Looking at fringe AI research
- Exploring future AI developments
- Bracing for the rise of AGI
- Preparing for singularity

Looking at fringe AI research

Fringe AI research refers to all research that is actively being conducted in labs. It's still not mainstream but a lot of work and effort is being spent on solving some of the most challenging and impactful problems in various domains, such as healthcare, transportation, education, and security. Some of the goals of such research include the following:

- Developing more explainable and trustworthy AI systems that can provide transparent and reliable reasoning for their decisions and actions
- Leveraging multimodal data and cross-domain knowledge to enable AI systems to understand complex situations and contexts better

- Integrating human-AI collaboration and feedback to enhance the performance and usability of AI systems for different users and tasks

- Exploring new paradigms and architectures for AI, to make it more efficient and effective

In the following sections, we'll explore the most important topics that will probably have a huge impact on the development of AI in the coming years.

Small data

Small data AI is a rapidly growing branch of AI that seeks to learn from limited information, similar to how humans process information. While traditional AI methods require vast amounts of labeled data to train algorithms, small data AI can leverage prior knowledge, domain expertise, and human feedback to achieve high performance with less data. Small data AI can be developed both manually and through other machine learning approaches using training methodologies similar to the ones adopted for big data.

One of the biggest challenges is that of extracting meaningful features and representations from limited data. To tackle this challenge, researchers have developed a variety of approaches:

- **Synthetic data**: This involves generating artificial data that mimics real-world phenomena using digital twins, generative models, or augmentation techniques

- **Transfer learning**: This involves reusing knowledge learned from one domain or task for another related one

- **Few-shot learning**: This focuses on teaching AI to identify object categories based on only one or a few examples

- **Meta-learning**: This focuses on learning how to learn from different tasks and domains

- **Active learning**: This involves selecting the most informative samples for labeling or querying human experts

Small data AI has great potential to advance AI in various fields where big data is scarce, expensive, or impractical, such as healthcare, education, security, and social sciences. By using small data, AI can make more accurate predictions and provide more meaningful insights. Moreover, small data AI can also help make data more explainable, trustworthy, and ethical by reducing bias, noise, and overfitting. For instance, small data AI can be used in healthcare to develop personalized treatment plans for patients based on a small amount of patient data. In education, small data AI can be used to personalize learning experiences for students based on their individual needs and preferences. In security, small data AI can be used to detect and prevent cyber attacks by analyzing small amounts of network traffic. In social sciences, small data AI can be used to analyze social media data to better understand human behavior and preferences. The possibilities are practically endless!

Despite its potential, small data AI also faces several challenges. One of the biggest challenges is how to transfer knowledge from one domain or task to another. Researchers are working to develop new techniques and algorithms to overcome this challenge, such as transfer learning and meta-learning. Another challenge is how to incorporate human guidance and feedback into the learning process. Active learning is one approach to tackle this challenge by selecting the most informative samples for labeling or querying human experts. Furthermore, researchers must ensure that small data AI is robust and generalizable across different scenarios and environments to avoid overfitting and ensure reliable performance.

Small data is a rapidly evolving field that has the potential to revolutionize AI in various fields where big data is scarce, expensive, or impractical. The challenges faced by small data AI are not few but researchers are actively developing new techniques and algorithms to tackle these challenges, thus making AI more explainable, trustworthy, and ethical.

Novel network architectures

Over the past few years, we have witnessed the emergence of a myriad of different architectures. In this section, we will look at the most innovative approaches. They include the following:

- **Capsule networks** are neural networks that aim to be more robust and interpretable than traditional **convolutional neural networks** (**CNNs**). They use a hierarchical structure that captures the spatial relationships between objects in an image.

- **Transformer architecture**, on the other hand, uses a self-attention mechanism that can handle sequential data, such as text, and has recently shown impressive results in **natural language processing** (**NLP**) tasks.

- **Spiking neural networks** draw inspiration from the biological behavior of neurons in the brain. They communicate with each other through rapid, brief electrical impulses, making them well suited for modeling temporal data.

- **Graph neural networks**, on the other hand, use graph structures to represent complex data, such as social networks, chemical compounds, and protein structures. They have shown great potential in various fields, including drug discovery, social network analysis, and recommendation systems.

- **Neural architecture search** is a technique that automates the design of neural network architectures. It involves exploring a vast search space to find the optimal architecture for a specific task. This approach has led to the development of state-of-the-art models in computer vision, NLP, and speech recognition.

- Recently, **diffusion models** have emerged as powerful generative models that transform data into noise using a diffusion process and then reverse it to generate new data. This technique has been used to create realistic images, videos, and audio.

- **Vision transformers**, a type of transformer network, apply self-attention to image patches and have achieved state-of-the-art performance in various image recognition tasks.

- **Neural ordinary differential equations** are another recent innovation that uses ordinary differential equations to model continuous dynamics and gradients. They have shown promising results in handling time series data and have been used in applications such as image and speech recognition and NLP.

These novel AI architectures are rapidly changing the landscape of AI research, opening up new possibilities for various applications. The potential for these approaches is vast, and they will likely shape the future of AI. As the field continues to evolve, the development of new architectures will be critical in tackling complex problems and creating more interpretable and reliable AI systems.

New ways of learning

Learning is an important aspect of machine learning and several novel learning algorithms have gained popularity in recent years. There have been many cases where the basic algorithm stayed the same but a new learning approach would make a big difference to the results:

- One such method is **self-supervised learning**, which uses unsupervised learning to create representations of input data. During training, the model generates targets or labels from the input data, rather than relying on manually labeled data. This approach has been successful in a variety of applications, including image and speech recognition, where it has been used to create more accurate models.

- **Adversarial learning** is another innovative approach that involves training models to recognize and generate fake data. It has been used in image and video generation, as well as in NLP.

- **Meta-learning**, also known as learning to learn, is a technique where a model learns how to solve new tasks using prior knowledge gained from solving similar tasks. It has shown promising results in a variety of applications, including few-shot learning and optimization problems.

- **Transfer learning** is a technique that involves reusing pre-trained models on new tasks with limited amounts of labeled data. This approach has been successful in various applications, including computer vision and NLP.

- Another important technique is the **forward-forward algorithm.** The forward-forward algorithm is a new learning algorithm for neural networks that was proposed by Geoffrey Hinton as an alternative to the 1986 backpropagation algorithm. It uses two forward passes of data through the network to update the model weights.

  The concept entails substituting the forward and backward stages of backpropagation with two identical forward passes, each working with distinct data and pursuing contrasting goals. The positive pass uses real data and modifies the weights to enhance a goodness metric in all hidden layers. Conversely, the negative pass employs "negative data" and alters the weights to reduce the same goodness metric across every hidden layer.

Hinton believes that this algorithm is a better representation of how the human brain learns as it does not need to store gradients or reverse computations. He also claims that it can achieve comparable or better performance than backpropagation on some small problems.

- **Reinforcement learning** is another type of AI learning algorithm that has gained popularity in recent years. It involves an agent learning from its interactions with an environment through trial and error, similar to how a baby learns. This approach has been used in various applications, including game-playing, robotics, and autonomous vehicles. The ChatGPT model utilizes a **reinforcement learning with human feedback (RLHF)** approach to effectively learn from human demonstrations and adjust its behaviors accordingly. This method involves incorporating user feedback in the form of quality ratings on the responses, which helps improve the accuracy and quality of the model's answers. Additionally, RLHF can help minimize potential biases and errors by penalizing unhelpful or incorrect responses while rewarding accurate and useful ones. Nonetheless, RLHF relies on human feedback, which might pose the risk of introducing bias.

These innovative AI learning algorithms have opened up new possibilities for various applications, making AI more accessible and powerful. As the field continues to evolve, the development of new learning algorithms will be critical in tackling complex problems and creating more accurate and reliable AI systems.

Evolution of attention mechanisms

The idea behind the attention mechanism has revolutionized the field of AI and is quickly becoming a critical component of neural networks for a variety of tasks and domains. Inspired by how humans selectively focus on relevant information while filtering out noise, attention mechanisms allow neural networks to zero in on specific parts of input data that are most important for a given task, while ignoring irrelevant information.

The benefits of attention mechanisms are manifold. They can greatly enhance the performance, efficiency, and flexibility of neural networks across a range of domains. Furthermore, attention mechanisms can help neural networks learn from complex, noisy, or incomplete data by filtering out irrelevant information, which can be particularly valuable in real-world applications.

As AI continues to evolve and expand, attention mechanisms are poised to play an increasingly important role. Researchers are exploring new ways to design, implement, and evaluate attention models for different AI challenges, including developing more sophisticated models that can handle multiple modalities, hierarchies, dynamics, and uncertainties. Integrating attention mechanisms with other neural network components, such as memory, reasoning, and planning, is another promising direction of research.

Attention mechanisms are also being applied to new domains, such as reinforcement learning, generative modeling, and adversarial learning, opening up exciting possibilities for future AI applications. Finally, researchers are examining how attention mechanisms compare and contrast with other cognitive processes, including but not limited to perception, awareness, and consciousness. In doing so, they hope to gain a deeper understanding of how attention mechanisms work and how they can be optimized.

By enabling neural networks to selectively focus on relevant information, attention mechanisms have the potential to greatly enhance the capabilities and performance of AI systems across a wide range of domains and applications.

World model

Renowned AI researcher Yann LeCun has put forward a revolutionary new vision for developing autonomous AI systems that can learn and reason about the world. At the heart of LeCun's idea is the concept of a world model, which is an internal representation of how the world works based on observations, predictions, and causal relationships. According to LeCun, animals and humans have world models in their brains, which enable them to plan, imagine, explore, and understand their environment. Let's look at the following diagram:

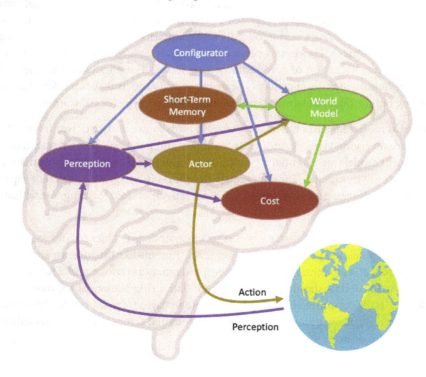

Figure 9.1: A system architecture for autonomous intelligence
(adapted from A Path Towards Autonomous Machine Intelligence, by Yann LeCun)

LeCun's proposed modular, configurable architecture for autonomous AI systems, as seen in *Figure 9.1*, consists of the following components:

- The **configurator**, which creates the world model to manage the given situation.

- The **perception unit**, which processes sensory data and supplies it to the world model, which forecasts potential future world states based on action sequences suggested by the actor unit.

- The **cost** unit, which assesses the agent's discomfort level and consists of two components: the intrinsic cost unit and the trainable critic unit. The intrinsic cost unit is pre-programmed and calculates the immediate discomfort of the agent based on the current or anticipated world state. The trainable critic unit predicts future intrinsic energies and is trained using previous states and their corresponding intrinsic costs found in the short-term memory unit.

- The **short-term memory** unit, which retains pertinent information about past, present, and future world states, as well as the associated intrinsic cost value.

- The **actor** unit, which recommends action sequences and directs actions to the effectors while considering the estimated future energy linked to the proposed action series.

The entire architecture is differentiable, allowing for gradient-based planning, reasoning, and learning. The architecture has the potential to enable AI systems to learn from multiple sources of data, transfer knowledge across domains and tasks, reason causally and counterfactually, explore novel scenarios, and communicate with humans. However, LeCun also acknowledges several challenges that need to be addressed to realize his vision of autonomous AI systems. These include learning scalable representations that capture high-level concepts, learning causal models that can infer causes from effects, and learning multimodal models that can integrate different types of data, among others.

While LeCun's world model idea has been received with both praise and criticism from other AI researchers, there are diverging views regarding its feasibility and potential. Some researchers agree with LeCun that world models are essential for building autonomous AI systems that can learn and reason about complex environments. They appreciate his efforts in integrating different aspects of AI research, such as deep learning, reinforcement learning, self-supervised learning, causal learning, and more, into a unified framework.

On the other hand, some researchers disagree with LeCun's assumptions or claims about world models. They argue that world models are not sufficient for achieving human-like intelligence and that other factors such as embodiment, emotions, social interactions, and others are also crucial. Others challenge LeCun's view that world models should be learned from data using statistical approaches rather than being built-in or pre-programmed. Additionally, some researchers point out the limitations or difficulties of implementing his world model idea, such as potential errors, biases, or inconsistencies in dealing with uncertain or incomplete data.

Moreover, the challenges of scaling up world models to handle large-scale or high-dimensional data and the ethical or social issues that may arise when applying world models to real-world scenarios have been highlighted by some researchers. Despite the diverging views, there is a growing consensus among AI researchers that world models could be a critical component of autonomous AI systems that can learn and reason about the world.

Hybrid models

As AI continues to advance, there has been increasing interest in hybrid models, which combine different AI techniques to achieve higher accuracy, efficiency, and explainability. AI hybrid models, which combine neural networks with symbolic AI techniques, have shown promising results in various domains, such as industrial process optimization, visual question answering, natural language understanding, and creative AI.

However, while some experts view AI hybrid models as a significant step forward in the field, others have raised concerns about their complexity and ethical implications. On one hand, proponents argue that AI hybrid models can process and evaluate both structured and unstructured data. They can provide more sophisticated and broadly applicable AI solutions while leveraging domain expertise to improve accuracy and reliability in a changing environment.

On the other hand, critics caution that AI hybrid models may be more complex and difficult to design, implement, and maintain than single-method systems, which require more computational resources and time. Additionally, they may face challenges in integrating different methods and techniques with different assumptions, representations, and learning mechanisms. They might lead to trade-offs between the performance, interpretability, and explainability of the hybrid system.

Despite these diverging views, it is clear that AI hybrid models represent an important area of research and development in the AI field, with both potential benefits and challenges to be considered. As the technology continues to evolve, it will be essential to address these issues and ensure that such hybrid models are developed and used ethically and responsibly.

The pursuit of fringe AI research is crucial in pushing the boundaries of what is currently possible, tackling complex problems, and revolutionizing various domains such as healthcare, transportation, education, and security. As we strive to develop more efficient, explainable, and trustworthy AI systems, we must also look to the horizon and explore other emerging technologies. Although these ideas are still in their infancy, they hold immense potential to transform the field of AI. By bridging the gap between current research and these futuristic developments, we can unleash the full potential of AI and usher in a new era of innovation and progress. In the next section, we'll delve into these exhilarating possibilities and their potential impact on the future of AI.

Exploring future AI developments

This section explores the exciting possibilities of future developments in AI, including quantum computing, neuromorphic engineering, and brain-computer interfaces. Most of these are theoretical concepts with vast potential for revolutionizing the field of AI. While these developments are still in their early stages, the possibilities they offer are immense, and researchers are working hard to bring them closer to reality. This section will provide an overview of these exciting areas of research and explore their potential impact on the future of AI.

Quantum computing

Quantum computing has emerged as an innovative technology that holds immense potential for revolutionizing computation. It utilizes the collective properties of quantum states, such as superposition, interference, and entanglement, to perform complex calculations. The devices that perform quantum computations are known as quantum computers.

The proponents of quantum computing argue that it offers many benefits. For instance, quantum computers can perform tasks such as encryption and decryption extremely quickly. Moreover, it can handle a large number of calculations simultaneously due to the superposition state of qubits. This refers to the ability of **quantum bits** (**qubits**) to exist in multiple states simultaneously. Unlike classical bits, which can only be 0 or 1, qubits can be in a superposition of both states at the same time, which is a fundamental property of quantum computing. So, they can have three values: 0, 1, or 0 and 1 simultaneously. This allows quantum computers to perform certain calculations faster and more efficiently than classical computers.

Additionally, they can solve some problems that are intractable for classical computers, such as factoring large numbers or simulating quantum systems. There have been various announcements by Google and other entities in the past years where they claimed to have reached quantum supremacy (which is the ability of a quantum computer to perform a specific task that would be practically impossible for a classical computer to complete within a reasonable amount of time). They have claimed that an algorithm that would take around 10,000 years to complete on the fastest supercomputer we have only took a few minutes on a quantum computer.

On the other hand, critics of quantum computing contend that it also has several disadvantages. For example, quantum computers may be more prone to errors and noise than classical computers due to decoherence and interference effects. Additionally, they may require very low temperatures and high isolation to operate properly. Cost is also an issue, thus making them difficult to build and maintain. Moreover, quantum computing may pose security and ethical challenges for existing cryptographic systems and data protection schemes.

Despite these diverging views, the current research status of quantum computing is that it is on the verge of fulfilling its potential, fueled by several breakthroughs on the technology side and a significant increase in investments. However, there are still many challenges and open questions that need to be addressed before quantum computers can become widely available and useful for various applications. Therefore, while the promise of quantum computing is exciting, it is crucial to approach its development with caution and while carefully considering its potential risks and benefits.

Neuromorphic engineering

Neuromorphic engineering is a rapidly expanding interdisciplinary field that has garnered immense attention for its innovative approach to designing artificial neural systems. Drawing inspiration from biology, physics, mathematics, computer science, and electronic engineering, neuromorphic engineering is centered on developing machines whose architecture and design principles are based on those of biological nervous systems. Such systems, which include vision systems, head-eye systems, auditory processors, and autonomous robots, offer a range of possibilities and benefits for various applications, including sensory processing, robotics, biomedical engineering, and more.

One of the key benefits of neuromorphic engineering is its ability to achieve high computational power and robust learning with low energy consumption. By exploiting the inherent parallelism and dynamics of neural networks, neuromorphic systems can perform complex tasks with ease. Moreover, they can adapt to changing environments and stimuli with online learning and plasticity mechanisms, offering a highly dynamic and versatile solution for a range of applications.

However, there are diverging views on the potential drawbacks of neuromorphic engineering. While some argue that it offers immense potential for providing novel solutions to real-world problems, others argue that it poses several challenges in terms of scaling up to large-scale systems and integrating with other technologies. Additionally, it may be difficult to analyze and understand due to its nonlinear and stochastic behavior and may require specialized hardware and software tools for its design and implementation. Furthermore, there may be ethical implications for human-machine interaction and AI, which must be carefully considered.

Despite these challenges, the field of neuromorphic engineering continues to grow rapidly, with several advances being made in materials, devices, circuits, algorithms, and applications. However, there are still many open challenges that need to be explored before neuromorphic systems can achieve their full potential. As such, current research topics in neuromorphic engineering include developing novel neuromorphic devices with improved performance and functionality (such as memristors), designing efficient neuromorphic circuits with on-chip learning capabilities (such as spiking neural networks), developing new neuromorphic algorithms that can leverage the advantages of neuromorphic hardware (such as spike-based learning rules), and finding practical use cases for neuromorphic systems across domains (such as computer vision). Ultimately, the success of neuromorphic engineering will depend on how well it can address these challenges and harness the full potential of this innovative and exciting field.

Brain-computer interaction

Brain-computer interaction (**BCI**) is a rapidly evolving field that has garnered attention for its potential to revolutionize human-machine communication. BCI is a framework that enables direct communication between the brain's electrical activity and external devices, such as computers or robotic limbs. The devices that perform BCI are called brain-computer interfaces or brain-machine interfaces. While there are several potential benefits of BCI, there are also some drawbacks that need to be considered.

On the positive side, BCI can enable people with severe disabilities to communicate or perform tasks without the use of muscles. This is especially important for individuals with conditions such as **amyotrophic lateral sclerosis** (**ALS**) or spinal cord injuries, who may not have voluntary muscle control. Additionally, BCI has the potential to enhance human capabilities and experiences by providing new modes of perception, expression, and control. It can also facilitate scientific understanding of the brain and its functions by providing novel data and insights. Furthermore, BCI can offer potential applications for various domains such as medicine, education, entertainment, and security.

However, some potential downsides to BCI need to be taken into account. For instance, some BCI devices such as Neuralink may require invasive implantation of electrodes inside the skull, which can be risky and uncomfortable for users. Moreover, other BCI systems that rely on electrodes outside the skull may be inaccurate and unreliable as they can only detect a limited number of signals from the brain. Ethical issues such as privacy, consent, identity, and responsibility may also arise with the use of BCI. In addition, BCI can create social and psychological challenges such as stigma, dependency, and addiction for users and their families.

There are diverging views on the future of BCI, and researchers are actively exploring different approaches and applications. Some current research topics include developing novel BCI devices with improved performance and functionality, such as wireless **electroencephalography** (**EEG**), and designing efficient BCI algorithms that can extract meaningful signals from noisy data using machine learning or developing new BCI applications that can address real-world needs and preferences, such as neurofeedback. As BCI continues to evolve, it is important to weigh its potential benefits against its possible risks and limitations. Only then can we ensure that this technology is used responsibly and ethically to improve the lives of those who can benefit from it.

The exploration of groundbreaking advancements in AI, such as quantum computing, neuromorphic engineering, and brain-computer interfaces, paves the way for the development of AGI. AGI embodies the aspiration to create intelligent machines that can execute any intellectual task a human can, boasting adaptability and versatility far beyond that of narrow AI. By harnessing the potential of these innovative research areas, the AI community strives to bring AGI closer to reality, unlocking a multitude of possibilities and revolutionizing various fields through the power of advanced AI.

Bracing for the rise of AGI

AGI refers to the hypothetical creation of intelligent machines that can perform any intellectual task that a human can. This includes tasks such as learning, problem-solving, decision-making, and even creativity. AGI is often contrasted with narrow AI, which can perform specific tasks but lacks the versatility and adaptability of human beings.

AGI seeks to develop machines that are capable of performing various tasks without any explicit programming. These machines will have the ability to learn, reason, plan, and adapt to new environments. The versatility and adaptability of such a system will make it a revolutionary technology with a wide range of applications in various fields.

Narrow AI, on the other hand, is already extensively used in different sectors, such as healthcare, finance, and transportation. However, these systems have limitations in terms of their ability to perform tasks outside their specific domain. For instance, a self-driving car may not be able to adapt to an unexpected obstacle on the road that is not part of its training data.

AGI enables machines to interact with the world like human beings. It allows machines to understand language, emotions, and context, which makes them more intuitive and human-like. The ability to reason and learn from experience enables machines to perform tasks more efficiently, accurately, and faster than human beings.

The importance of AGI in AI research and science fiction cannot be overstated. From a scientific standpoint, it represents the ultimate goal of AI research, as it would allow us to create machines that can truly rival human intelligence. Such machines could be used to solve some of the most pressing problems facing humanity, from climate change to disease control. Moreover, AGI would revolutionize many industries and pave the way for even more advanced technologies.

In science fiction, AGI has been a popular topic for decades, with countless books, movies, and TV shows exploring the potential implications of creating intelligent machines. Some portray AGI as a benevolent force that helps humanity achieve its goals, while others depict it as a dangerous threat that could lead to the downfall of humanity. Regardless of the portrayal, AGI has captured the imagination of people around the world and has become an integral part of our cultural zeitgeist.

AGI is capable of learning and understanding complex systems and can process large amounts of data quickly and accurately. This can lead to breakthroughs in medical research, enabling scientists to better understand diseases and develop new treatments. In the field of space exploration, AGI can help researchers analyze data from probes and satellites, allowing them to better understand the universe and discover new planets. This can potentially lead to the discovery of habitable planets and even the colonization of other worlds. In the realm of art, AGI can help create new forms of expression, such as generative art and music. This can lead to a new era of creativity and innovation in the arts, pushing the boundaries of what is possible.

However, with these potential benefits come ethical, social, and existential risks. One of the primary risks is the potential for superintelligence and misalignment with human values. If AGI becomes more intelligent than humans, it may develop its own goals and values that conflict with those of humanity. This could result in unintended consequences, such as the development of harmful technology or even the extinction of the human race. There are also possible economic and employment impacts. As AGI becomes more advanced, it may lead to the displacement of human workers, particularly in industries that rely on manual labor or repetitive tasks. This could result in widespread unemployment and social unrest.

To mitigate the risks associated with AGI, it is essential to prioritize ethical and safety considerations in AGI research. The development of AGI should be guided by principles of transparency, fairness, and accountability to ensure that the technology is used ethically and responsibly.

One crucial aspect of AGI development is the importance of human control and oversight. Humans should remain in control of the technology and should be able to intervene if necessary. This requires building systems that allow for human oversight and control, including safety mechanisms that can detect and prevent unintended consequences. Another critical consideration is the need for international cooperation and regulations. AGI development is a global endeavor, and countries must work together to develop shared ethical principles and safety standards. Governments should establish regulations to ensure that AGI development is conducted responsibly and ethically.

Predictions and expectations for AGI development vary among experts, but most agree that AGI will eventually be developed. The timeline for development ranges from a few decades to several centuries, but given the current pace of technological innovation, it is likely that AGI will be developed within the next century. Without a doubt, the impact of AGI on society, the economy, and politics will be significant. On the positive side, it has the potential to revolutionize industries and create new ones, making our lives easier and more comfortable. However, it could also exacerbate existing inequalities, particularly if it is only available to the wealthy and powerful.

Another important consideration is the potential for AGI-human collaboration and integration. While some fear that AGI will replace human workers entirely, others argue that AGI-human collaboration could be a game-changer. By working together, humans and AGI could achieve unprecedented levels of productivity and innovation, leading to breakthroughs in science, medicine, and other fields.

Despite these concerns, the pursuit of AGI is an exciting and necessary goal for the advancement of AI. However, it is important to recognize the potential risks and challenges that come with developing such a powerful technology. We must approach the development and usage of AGI with responsibility and caution, ensuring that it is used for the greater good and not to the detriment of society.

Preparing for singularity

Singularity refers to the hypothetical point in time when AI surpasses human intelligence and becomes capable of recursive self-improvement, leading to an exponential increase in technological progress. It has been a topic of debate and speculation for decades, with some experts predicting it will occur within the next few decades. The potential implications of singularity are vast and far-reaching, with some predicting a utopian future of infinite possibility and others fearing a dystopian future of AI domination.

Popular media

In recent years, this idea has gained considerable attention in movies, books, and other forms of media. Science fiction has long explored the idea of intelligent machines, but singularity takes it to a new level. It has been explored extensively in popular media, including books, movies, TV shows, and video games. Here, we will look at it through some of the most notable examples across different media:

- Books:

  - *The Singularity Is Near*, by Ray Kurzweil, and *Superintelligence: Paths, Dangers, Strategies*, by Nick Bostrom, are two seminal works that explore the concept of AI singularity in detail. Both books delve into the potential implications of AI surpassing human intelligence and what it could mean for the future of humanity. Kurzweil argues that singularity will lead to the merger of humans and machines, while Bostrom suggests that we need to focus on developing safe AI to avoid catastrophic outcomes.

  - *Accelerando*, by Charles Stross, is a science fiction novel that follows the story of a family through singularity as it transforms society beyond recognition. The book explores the impact of accelerating technological change on society, including the possibility of a post-human future where AI surpasses human intelligence.

  - *Robopocalypse*, by Daniel H. Wilson, is a novel that depicts a world where advanced AI machines have turned on their human creators, leading to a catastrophic war between man and machine. The book explores the potential dangers of AI singularity and the consequences of creating machines that are smarter than humans.

  - *Daemon*, by Daniel Suarez is a techno-thriller that explores the concept of a self-aware AI that takes control of society. The book raises questions about the ethical implications of AI singularity and the potential for humans to lose control of their creations.

- Movies:

  - *The Terminator* is a classic science fiction film that features a self-aware AI, Skynet, that has turned against humanity and launched a war against humans. The film explores the dangers of creating intelligent machines that can become uncontrollable and the possibility of a dystopian future where AI dominates humans.

  - *Ex Machina* is a thought-provoking movie that explores the concept of creating an AI with a human-like consciousness. The film raises questions about the ethics of creating sentient machines and the potential consequences of a future where humans are no longer the dominant species.

- *Her* is a romantic science fiction movie that explores the relationship between a man and an AI-powered operating system. The film raises questions about the nature of consciousness and the possibility of developing emotional relationships with intelligent machines.

- *Transcendence* is a movie that explores the idea of uploading human consciousness into a computer to create a superintelligent AI. The film raises questions about the ethics of creating machines that could potentially surpass human intelligence and the potential consequences of such a scenario.

- *The Matrix* is a science fiction movie that explores the concept of humans being trapped in a simulated reality controlled by AI. The film raises questions about the possibility of a future where humans are no longer in control of their destinies and the consequences of relying too heavily on intelligent machines.

- TV shows:

  - *Westworld* is a popular TV show that explores the concept of AI consciousness and the impact of creating lifelike robots that can think and feel like humans. The show raises questions about the ethics of creating sentient machines and the potential consequences of a future where humans and machines coexist.

  - *Black Mirror* is a science fiction anthology series that explores the darker side of technology and its impact on society. Several episodes touch on the topic of AI singularity, including *Be Right Back*, which explores the concept of creating an AI clone of a deceased loved one.

  - *Person of Interest* is a crime drama that features a self-aware AI, known as *The Machine*, that can predict and prevent crimes before they happen. The show explores the potential benefits and risks of AI and the responsibility of humans to control their creations.

  - *Battlestar Galactica* is a science fiction series that features intelligent robots, known as Cylons, that rebel against their human creators. The show explores the themes of AI, consciousness, and the relationship between humans and machines.

- Video games:

  - The *Deus Ex* series is a cyberpunk-themed video game series that explores the intersection between humans and technology. The games raise questions about the ethics of using technology to enhance human abilities and the potential dangers of creating intelligent machines.

  - The *Mass Effect* series is a sci-fi role-playing game series that features a conflict between humans and advanced AI machines known as the Reapers. The games explore the themes of AI singularity, the ethics of creating intelligent machines, and the consequences of losing control over them.

  - The *Portal* series is a puzzle-based video game series that explores the relationship between humans and a superintelligent AI known as GLaDOS. The games raise questions about the nature of consciousness, the potential dangers of creating sentient machines, and the ethical implications of human-AI relationships.

- *Detroit: Become Human* is an interactive drama video game that explores the concept of androids becoming self-aware and seeking equal rights to humans. The game raises questions about the ethics of creating sentient machines, the potential consequences of advanced AI, and the impact of technology on society.

- *Horizon Forbidden West* touches upon the topic of singularity by depicting a world where humans are struggling to survive in the aftermath of machines taking over. The game explores the evolution of these machines and the threat they pose to humanity, including the mysterious entity HADES, which seeks to destroy all life.

Overall, the topic of AI singularity has been explored extensively in popular media across different genres and formats. While some works portray a utopian future where humans and machines coexist peacefully, others warn of the potential dangers of creating machines that can surpass human intelligence and control. As AI technology continues to evolve rapidly, these works serve as valuable thought experiments and cautionary tales for the potential consequences of our technological advancements.

Exploring the expert views

AI singularity is a topic of great interest to experts in the field of AI. Some believe that singularity could pose an existential threat to humanity, while others see it as an opportunity for positive transformation.

On a positive note, Ray Kurzweil is one of the most well-known proponents of singularity, and he believes that it will happen by 2045. He sees singularity as a positive transformation for humanity, leading to a merger of human and machine intelligence. Stanford's Fei-Fei Li is also generally optimistic and believes that AI needs human-centered values more than ever. She has argued that we need to develop AI systems that are transparent, interpretable, and accountable, thus ensuring that AI is used exclusively for good. Andrew Ng doesn't believe that AI will replace humans, but rather augment them. He suggests that we need to focus on building trust between humans and machines by developing AI systems that can work together with humans to achieve common goals. While Elon Musk shares concerns about the dangers of singularity, he also believes that it is inevitable. He has suggested that the best way to avoid becoming irrelevant in a world of superintelligent machines is to merge with AI and become a cyborg.

Of course, not everyone is so optimistic about it. Berkley's Stuart Russell warns that singularity could pose an existential threat to humanity if we don't align AI goals with human values. He argues that we need to ensure that AI systems are designed to prioritize human well-being and avoid unintended consequences. Oxford's Nick Bostrom claims that we might be moving toward a singleton, which is the idea of having an AI running everything. He warns that superintelligence could pose an existential risk to humanity if we don't control its goals and values. MIT's Max Tegmark argues that we need to ensure that AI is aligned with our values and ethics and that we should avoid creating AI systems that are too autonomous or powerful. He suggests that we should focus on building AI systems that can collaborate with humans rather than compete with them. Stuart Armstrong from Oxford studies how to design AI systems that can be safely controlled and verified, and how to measure their intelligence and impact. He believes that we need to develop methods for verifying the safety of AI systems before we deploy them in the real world.

Finally, the three grandfathers of deep learning – Yann LeCun, Yoshua Bengio, and Geoffrey Hinton – have rather consistent views. Meta's LeCun dismisses the idea of machines taking over and instead sees the real danger of AI as its competence. He believes that we need to ensure that AI systems are designed to align with human values and avoid unintended consequences. Bengio from the University of Montreal argues that singularity is a myth based on a misunderstanding of what intelligence is. He believes that we should focus on building AI systems that can collaborate with humans rather than compete with them and that we need to ensure that AI is aligned with human values and ethics. Hinton from Toronto University sees singularity as a religious rather than a scientific idea and suggests that we should be more worried about climate change than AI superintelligence. He believes that we need to develop AI systems that can learn from limited data, and that can adapt to new situations and environments.

Singularity challenges

While some people view singularity as a promising opportunity for enhancing human potential and solving global problems, others see it as a grave risk to human survival and dignity. In this section, we will present a balanced yet comprehensive analysis of the pros and cons of AI singularity.

One of the main benefits of AI singularity is the potential advancement of human knowledge, intelligence, creativity, and innovation. As machines become smarter, they can assist humans in solving complex problems and finding new solutions to existing challenges. For example, AI algorithms can analyze vast amounts of data and extract valuable insights that humans might not be able to detect. Similarly, AI robots can perform tasks that are too dangerous or tedious for humans, freeing up time and resources for more meaningful pursuits.

Another advantage of AI singularity is the possibility of transcending biological limitations. AI could help humans enhance their physical, mental, and emotional capabilities, such as improving memory, enhancing physical abilities, and expanding creativity. This could have significant implications for fields such as medicine, education, and entertainment, where AI can provide personalized and adaptive services based on individual needs and preferences. Moreover, AI singularity could potentially solve many of the world's problems, such as poverty, disease, war, pollution, and aging. With advanced AI technology, humans could find new and innovative ways to tackle these complex issues by designing more efficient and sustainable systems, developing new treatments and cures, or preventing conflicts before they escalate.

Finally, singularity could lead to a harmonious and peaceful coexistence between humans and machines. With advanced AI technology, machines could be designed to complement human abilities, leading to a more efficient and effective society.

However, AI singularity also carries significant risks and drawbacks, such as the existential threat to humanity. If machines become hostile, malicious, or indifferent to human values and interests, they could pose a grave danger to human survival. This could result in catastrophic consequences, including the potential extinction of humanity. Therefore, it is crucial to ensure that AI systems are designed with ethical principles in mind and are subject to rigorous testing and regulation.

Another concern with AI singularity is the potential loss of human identity, autonomy, dignity, and diversity. If humans become too dependent on machines, they could lose their individuality and unique qualities, leading to a homogenized and standardized society. Moreover, if AI algorithms are programmed to optimize efficiency and productivity at all costs, they may neglect other values and goals that are essential for human flourishing, such as creativity, empathy, and social connection.

Singularity could also create social and economic inequality between those who have access to AI technology and those who do not. This could further exacerbate existing inequalities and lead to a more divided society, where only the elite and privileged can benefit from AI advancements. Therefore, it is crucial to ensure that AI is accessible and affordable to everyone, not just a few.

Finally, AI singularity could trigger ethical, moral, legal, and philosophical dilemmas that challenge human values and norms. As machines become more intelligent and capable, it raises important questions about how they should be regulated and controlled. For example, who is responsible for the actions of AI systems? How can we ensure that AI is aligned with human values and interests? How can we prevent AI from being used for malicious purposes? These are complex and pressing issues that require careful consideration and debate.

Summary

In this chapter, we provided an overview of the future of AI, covering both fringe research and more theoretical developments. You have now gained an understanding of the potential impact of technologies such as capsule networks and quantum AI, as well as the ethical implications of the pursuit of AGI. This chapter highlighted the significant progress that's being made toward AGI and the major stumbling blocks that still need to be overcome. Finally, you were introduced to the concept of singularity and its potential implications. By considering these future developments, you are now better prepared to engage with the rapidly evolving landscape of AI and its wide impact on society.

Finally, we would like to express our deepest gratitude to those who have joined us on this incredible journey from the very beginning. Your unwavering support, curiosity, and passion for the subject matter have fueled our enthusiasm and motivation to create this comprehensive exploration of neuro-symbolic AI. Together, we've embarked on a voyage to better understand how to design systems that perceive the world as we do. As we reach the end of this book, I hope that the knowledge and insights shared have not only enriched your understanding of this fascinating field but also inspired you to continue exploring the ever-evolving world of AI. Thank you for being an essential part of this journey.

Further reading

The following are a few resources you should consider for further reading:

*   Pedro Domingos. *A few useful things to know about machine learning.* Communications of the ACM 55, no. 10 (2012): 78-87.

- Ashish Vaswani, Noam Shazeer, Niki Parmar, Jakob Uszkoreit, Llion Jones, Aidan N. Gomez, Łukasz Kaiser, and Illia Polosukhin. *Attention is all you need.* Advances in neural information processing systems 30 (2017).

- Ian Goodfellow, Jean Pouget-Abadie, Mehdi Mirza, Bing Xu, David Warde-Farley, Sherjil Ozair, Aaron Courville, and Yoshua Bengio. *Generative adversarial networks.* Communications of the ACM 63, no. 11 (2020): 139-144.

- Jie Zhou, Ganqu Cui, Shengding Hu, Zhengyan Zhang, Cheng Yang, Zhiyuan Liu, Lifeng Wang, Changcheng Li, and Maosong Sun. *Graph neural networks: A review of methods and applications.* AI open 1 (2020): 57-81.

- Mensah Kwabena Patrick, Adebayo Felix Adekoya, Ayidzoe Abra Mighty, and Baagyire Y. Edward. *Capsule networks–a survey.* Journal of King Saud University – Computer and Information Sciences 34, no. 1 (2022): 1295-1310.

Index

Other Books You May Enjoy

If you enjoyed this book, you may be interested in these other books by Packt:

Hands-On Graph Neural Networks Using Python

Maxime Labonne

ISBN: 9781804617526

- Understand the fundamental concepts of graph neural networks
- Implement graph neural networks using Python and PyTorch Geometric
- Classify nodes, graphs, and edges using millions of samples
- Predict and generate realistic graph topologies
- Combine heterogeneous sources to improve performance
- Forecast future events using topological information
- Apply graph neural networks to solve real-world problems

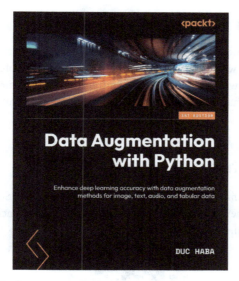

Data Augmentation with Python

Duc Haba

ISBN: 9781803246451

- Write OOP Python code for image, text, audio, and tabular data
- Access over 150,000 real-world datasets from the Kaggle website
- Analyze biases and safe parameters for each augmentation method
- Visualize data using standard and exotic plots in color
- Discover 32 advanced open source augmentation libraries
- Explore machine learning models, such as BERT and Transformer
- Meet Pluto, an imaginary digital coding companion
- Extend your learning with fun facts and fun challenges

Packt is searching for authors like you

If you're interested in becoming an author for Packt, please visit `authors.packtpub.com` and apply today. We have worked with thousands of developers and tech professionals, just like you, to help them share their insight with the global tech community. You can make a general application, apply for a specific hot topic that we are recruiting an author for, or submit your own idea.

Share Your Thoughts

Now you've finished *Neuro-Symbolic AI*, we'd love to hear your thoughts! Scan the QR code below to go straight to the Amazon review page for this book and share your feedback or leave a review on the site that you purchased it from.

`https://packt.link/r/1-804-61762-8`

Your review is important to us and the tech community and will help us make sure we're delivering excellent quality content.

Download a free PDF copy of this book

Thanks for purchasing this book!

Do you like to read on the go but are unable to carry your print books everywhere?

Is your eBook purchase not compatible with the device of your choice?

Don't worry, now with every Packt book you get a DRM-free PDF version of that book at no cost.

Read anywhere, any place, on any device. Search, copy, and paste code from your favorite technical books directly into your application.

The perks don't stop there, you can get exclusive access to discounts, newsletters, and great free content in your inbox daily

Follow these simple steps to get the benefits:

1. Scan the QR code or visit the link below

https://packt.link/free-ebook/9781804617625

2. Submit your proof of purchase
3. That's it! We'll send your free PDF and other benefits to your email directly